EXPRESS YOURSELF!

The essential guide to international understanding

Michael Powell

INSIDERS' GUIDE®

Published in North America by The Globe Pequot Press
Copyright © 2007 by Gusto Company AS under license to JW Cappelens forlag
www.gusto.tv
Written by Michael Powell
Original concept by Michael Powell, James Tavendale and Ernesto Gremese
Edited by Royce Meyer

10 9 8 7 6 5 4 3 2 1

Layout: Allen Boe
Photo credits: Getty Images

ISBN: 978-0-7627-4484-8

Library of Congress Cataloging-in-Publication Data is available on file.

Printed and manufactured in China

First Edition/First Printing

EXPRESS YOURSELF!

The essential guide to international understanding

Contents

EXPRESS YOURSELF!

The essential guide to international understanding

Introduction

"The real voyage of discovery consists not in seeing new landscapes, but in having new eyes."
Marcel Proust

For the inexperienced traveler, being abroad can be physically as well as mentally challenging. It quickly becomes apparent that connecting with people from other places requires a lot more than packing a phrase book and then waving your arms wildly from the first moment you step off the airplane.

Whether you are trekking across the Andes on a yak or soaking in a volcanic Icelandic spa, every society you encounter will have a unique and intricate repertoire of acceptable and unacceptable behaviors, facial and body gestures (or lack of them), and subtle ways of expressing or concealing thoughts and emotions. What is more, these social codes play out against a historical backdrop that has shaped each country's culture and national character over thousands of years.

This book won't turn you into a mind-reader overnight, but it will give an insight into what makes people tick in forty-five countries around the world. It will help you to keep your feet firmly on the ground in more ways than one (and tell you why in some places baring your soles is a big turn-off); it will make you smile (and advise you when to keep a straight face); it will even show you how to give other people a good giggle, which has got to be one of surest ways to break down cultural barriers. Beware though! If you think you can get by with a cheery grin and a handful of wisecracks, think again. Did you know that in some countries an unsuitable one-liner is punishable by death? Now that's no laughing matter.

So what's the secret of expressing yourself abroad? What separates the artful expat from the gawkish globetrotter, the lost soul from the life and soul? Well, for starters, the best way to foster an interest in foreign cultures and to really connect with other human beings, to open many doors (rather than having them slammed in your face), is to remember that while on the whole we are much more similar than we are different:

DO NOT ASSUME THAT EVERYONE ELSE IS JUST LIKE YOU!

From making an excellent first impression to building lasting friendships, Express Yourself! gives you the confidence to know that whenever you speak your icebreakers won't cause a diplomatic scene, whatever you do your body language will blend in with the group, and wherever you go you will always receive a warm welcome.

DISCLAIMER: Information about medical precautions (such as inoculations) and whether the countries included in this book are safe to visit is not included in this book, since this information is subject to change. If in doubt, always check with your embassy before traveling.

Argentina

National character

Argentina is one of the most prosperous and European countries in Latin America, and its capital, Buenos Aires, is very cosmopolitan; dress well there if you want to be taken seriously (the countryside is more relaxed). Argentines are quite serious and formal with strangers, but they are very family-oriented and relationships are paramount.

Argentines are quite conservative and risk averse—and bureaucracy is notorious—although time keeping is relaxed, so expect to be kept waiting before business appointments. You should be on time for restaurant reservations, but it is polite to be thirty minutes or more late for parties or dinner invitations at someone's home. Argentines also tend to enjoy each other's company over a cup of bitter tea called "mate." Don't ever refuse the offer of a cup, or you'll come across as rude.

A brief history

Before the arrival of Spanish settlers in the early sixteenth century, the most advanced indigenous culture in Argentina was the

Diaguita people. In 1580, Spain established a colony on the site of Buenos Aires, which became a thriving port and one of the most significant commercial centers of the area. During the nineteenth century the struggle for independence was led by General Jose de San Martin, who is remembered in Argentina as one of the Liberators of Spanish South America. Argentina declared its indepen dence on July 9, 1816, calling itself the United Provinces of Río de la Plata, but fighting broke out between its various provinces, so it wasn't fully united until 1880.

The War of the Triple Alliance was fought between Argentina, Brazil, and Uruguay against Paraguay. An economic revolution took place in the late nineteenth century, as the country secured significant European (especially British) investment, and increased its agricultural exports. After World War II, Army Colonel Juan Domingo Péron led a coup to become the country's leader, and was elected three times during the next thirty years. Supporters of Péron and his wife, Eva, argued he was trying to eliminate poverty and champion the working class, while his enemies saw him as a dictator. After his death in 1974, the country suffered economic downfall and brutal suppression of its people from the ruling military junta. In 1982 Argentina suffered defeat by the UK in the Falklands War, and returned to democracy soon afterwards. The economy all but collapsed between 2001 and 2002, leading to riots and depreciation of the currency to one-quarter of its former value. Today Argentina's economy is recovering very quickly, although political and economic corruption is still endemic.

Speaking
The national language, Spanish, which the Argentines call "Castellano," is heavily influenced by Italian, and is unlike the Spanish spoken elsewhere in Latin America. The most striking and rather quaint example of this is the pronoun "vos" which replaces the informal you (tú) pronoun, and is akin to saying "thee." Many people speak English, and there are about 1.5 million Italian speakers.

Titles are significant, especially among the elderly. Address a PhD or doctor as Doctor, a teacher as Professor, a lawyer as Abogado, etc. Those without professional titles are Mr. (Señor), Mrs. (Señora), and Miss (Señorita).

Body language
Even though South American countries have a reputation for being laid-back, Argentines are quite serious and sophisticated. Maintain good posture, and keep your hands out of your pockets. Do not yawn or stretch in public.

When greeting for the first time you should shake hands and nod, but with closer friends you may be greeted with a kiss on the right cheek, or even an embrace. Close male friends often take part in an abrazo—the act of a firm handshake, followed by a hug with much backslapping, and then another handshake.

Personal space is small. Argentines stand close, and they may even place their hand on your shoulder, but don't back away; they will think you are being shy (or worse, unfriendly) and will quickly close the gap. Even at this close distance, you should always maintain good eye contact.

Rocking the right hand a few times, palm facing upward, while keeping the fingers together at an angle means, "What's going on?" or "I don't understand."

A sweeping gesture beginning under the chin and continuing up over the top of the head means "I don't know" or "I don't care."

With thumb and middle finger touching, tapping them with the index finger means "Hurry up" or "Much."

You may hear an Argentine attracting a waiter's attention by making a kissing noise. Don't copy this rather unmannerly gesture, especially in upscale restaurants. Instead, raise your hand discreetly with your index finger extended. If you host the meal, you should pick up the tab. If you are a guest, it is polite to offer to pay, but don't argue the point too far.

Keep your hands visible on the table when dining, not in your lap.

Avoid talking about politics, Brazil and Chile (Argentina's archrivals), or the Falklands War. Safe topics include soccer (fútbol), tango, opera, restaurants, and sightseeing.

Sense of humor

Argentine banter can contain gentle put-downs and criticisms—a recent commercial tauntingly highlighted the fact that Carlos Tevez, named the top player in the Brazilian league, is an Argentine—as well as flirtations—"Diosa!" (Goddess!)—so take it as a sign that the company is relaxed enough to joke around with you, rather than be offended.

Many jokes in Argentina revolve around wordplay or refer to strange pronunciation in other languages and often begin with the phrase "Cómo se dice...?" (How do you say...?). Galicians (Spanish), Americans, and the English are popular targets. Political humor is popular on TV. Argentine youth enjoy phone pranks. One of the first popular prank-callers in Argentina was "Doctor Tangalanga."

 # Australia

National character

Australian society is fiercely egalitarian. The "tall poppy" syndrome is a feature of Australian culture, referring to the way that those who boast about their abilities or think that they are better than everyone else are quickly brought down to size, usually with humor. Australians are laid-back but direct communicators, who respect honesty and down-to-earth interaction. They are very open to innovation and new ideas and are not risk-averse. Independence and self-reliance are held in high esteem, which makes them quite hard nosed and objective rather than emotional. They are naturally accepting and trusting unless given good evidence to the contrary

A brief history

The original inhabitants of Australia, the Aborigines, were hunter-gatherers who arrived 40,000 years ago, when an ice age connected Australia and Asia by a land bridge.

In 1770, Captain Cook of England arrived in Botany Bay and claimed the whole of Australia (then known as New South Wales) for Britain, because the country was judged to be a terra nullius, or empty land. Penal colonies were quickly established and thousands of convicts were shipped there from Great Britain. The first shipment of eleven ships set sail from Portsmouth on May 13, 1787, with 759 convicts on board. They landed at Port Jackson on January 26, 1788. The first free settlers arrived in 1793 and numbers increased following the discovery of gold in 1851 by British prospector Edward Hammond Hargraves. The Europeans drove the Aborigines off their land.

In 1797 Merino sheep were brought to Australia. The number of sheep in Australia quickly increased to more than a million within thirty years.

Australia joined the British Commonwealth on January 1, 1901, and in 1942 the Statute of Westminster Adoption Act gave the country complete autonomy over its own affairs. Seven years later, the National Citizenship Act made Australians official citizens of Australia—no longer citizens of the UK and surrounding colonies as they had been before.

In 1992 the Mabo Judgment overturned the doctrine of terra nullius and gave Aborigines the right to use some of the government-owned land. While this is undoubtedly a very important step towards the achievement of justice in Australia, many Aborigines feel that the judgment will have little real impact on their long-term rights, since the damage to their communities has already been done.

Speaking

Most Australians speak English, but they like to abbreviate or shorten words and use an extensive repertoire of slang and idiom. This way of communicating can be somewhat confusing to British or American English speakers. Conversation is direct; Australians say what is on their minds. Unfortunately, this may make Australians come across as blunt and insensitive but that's not the case. They simply prefer brevity and directness to flowery language full of detail and digressions. Good-natured banter and humor are a natural part of Australian communication, even in business.

Australians are friendly and easy to get to know, but will mock those who try to impress, especially with academic qualifications. If they disagree with you they will say so, but they will also respect your own strong opinions—even if they differ from their own—so long as you express yourself with honesty and candor.

Body language

Many indigenous Australians believe it is impolite to look you in the eye, whereas non-indigenous Australians use eye contact that is direct and firm—indicative of honesty, attention, and sincerity.

Personal body space is quite wide, so allow at least two feet of space.

Australian men are not very tactile with each other, so don't put your arm around another man or engage in any other physical "buddy" behavior unless you know him very well. Australian women are about as tactile as women from Northern Europe.

Sense of humor

Australian humor is often black, making jokes about tragedies as a way of coping with them. For example, in 1967, Prime Minister Harold Holt went for a swim at a Portsea beach and was never seen again. As a result, the Harold Holt Memorial Swimming Pool was built in his honor.

To make a joke at a friend's expense is a sign of a healthy friendship. If you are teased, you are expected to stand up for yourself and reply in kind, with good humor, rather than take offense.

Austria

National character

Austrians are very polite and quite formal, and place great importance on showing courtesy and respect to each other, especially to one's elders and superiors. There is also a strong need for consensus, observing the correct protocol, and being punctual.

Community and social consciousness plays an important role in Austrian society. Austrians also share a deep respect for order and the rule of law. They are direct in their speech and their dealings. They value objective facts, logic, and reason above emotion but their conservative nature means that sudden change is unwelcome.

Many Austrians feel profoundly linked to nature and the environment. They enjoy experiencing the great outdoors and everything it has to offer, including skiing, hiking, and camping.

A brief history

Settled in prehistoric times, the area that is now Austria was occupied by the Celts, and later by the Romans. After the fall of the Roman Empire, the area became part of Charlemagne's Empire. In 1278, the Habsburg king, Rudolph, seized Austria. His dynasty continued to rule Austria for the next 640 years, until the defeat of Austria-Hungary in World War I.

On November 12, 1918, Austria became a republic called German Austria and tried unsuccessfully to gain union with Germany. However, under the Christian Social Party, the Austrian government moved towards centralization of power in the Fascist model. In 1933, Chancellor Engelbert Dolfuss established a dictatorship to check the power of Austrian Nazis, but he was assassinated on July 25, 1934. Four years later, the country was annexed by Germany's Third Reich.

After World War II, the U.S. and Britain liberated Austria, but the Russians remained there for another ten years. Finally Austria made a treaty with the USSR promising to remain neutral during the Cold War and reestablished its independence on May 15, 1955. Today the country has tough laws against Nazi propaganda, and recently the British historian David Irving spent thirteen months in jail for saying there were no gas chambers in Auschwitz. Austria joined the European Union on January 1, 1995.

Speaking

The official language of Austria is German, although French, Italian, and English are also spoken and are studied at school.

When entering a shop or restaurant, you should smile and acknowledge everyone by saying "Grüß Gott" (God bless you/Greet God, pronounced greuse got). Even when walking down the street, you may be greeted in the same way, to which you should reply, "Grüß Gott," or "Grüß dich" (pronounced greuse dikh) more informally, or to a child.

Small talk is very important. Expect to be asked about your journey or what you think about some of the scenic Austrian places you have visited. Small talk also serves as lively and philosophical debate, and so you may well be asked your opinion of current events. Austrian culture is distinct from that of Germany, so don't make the mistake of lumping them together. Always try to show that you know a little about Austrian culture and history (such as its architecture—some of Austria's most famous castles include the Burg Hohenwerfen, Castle Liechtenstein, and the Schloß Artstetten—and it has a rich musical heritage: Vienna was the European capital of classical music during the eighteenth and nineteenth centuries). Always maintain good eye contact while speaking, or you will be considered untrustworthy. Directness and honesty are important, so don't make promises or extend invitations unless you intend to follow them through.

Body language

You should always try to greet by shaking hands (even children) and maintaining good eye contact. However, only shake hands with a woman if she offers hers first. When you become better acquainted a handshake may be replaced with air kisses above both cheeks. Shake hands again on leaving and say "Auf Wiedersehen" (Until we see each other again, pronounced aahwf-vee-der-sayn).

When eating, keep your hands visible on top of the table, not in your lap, but keep your elbows off the table.

When making a toast, raise a glass and say, "Prost" (meaning "cheers"). It is vital to maintain eye contact, otherwise you will be considered rude.

Keep your hands out of your pockets, or you will be viewed as socially awkward, or even insulting. Try to maintain a simple open posture, with your hands by your sides rather than folded, or on your hips.

Sense of humor

Austrian humor is subtle, self-deprecating, ironical, and sometimes dark, as demonstrated by one of the most successful and respected comedians in Austria, Josef Hader. It aims to elicit a wry chuckle rather than a belly laugh (which would be seen as distasteful). Famous examples of Austrian wit include: "There is nothing so entertaining as the discussion of a book nobody has read" and "Do not learn more than you absolutely need to get through life."

Belgium

National character

The north and south of Belgium are almost two separate countries. The north, called Flanders, is primarily Dutch-speaking. The south, called Wallonia, is French-speaking. There is also a small area of German speakers in the east. While this means that Belgians have what some would call a crisis of identity, their culture is very diverse and they value common sense and the willingness to compromise. They have an egalitarian and anti-authoritarian culture, despite their apparent formality.

Belgians may appear shy, private, and formal at first meeting, but they have a strong humanitarian outlook that is masked by a pragmatic and calm outward appearance. Once a relationship has been developed Belgians will become more informal and relaxed.

A brief history

Throughout its history Belgium had been repeatedly invaded by other countries. The earliest named inhabitants of Belgium were a Celtic tribe called the Belgae, which spoke an Indo-European language intermediate between Celtic and Germanic. It became part of the Roman Empire in 50 B.C. until it was overrun by the Frankish invaders in the fifth century. After the decline of the Holy Roman Empire in the eleventh and twelfth centuries, the area was divided into independent feudal states.

In the sixteenth century, Belgium and the Netherlands were ruled by Spain. Together, they were known as the Spanish Netherlands (the Dutch later broke away to form the Dutch Republic). In 1713 Belgium fell into the control of Austria, and later became part of France. After the defeat of Napoleon in 1815, Belgium was given to the Netherlands, but broke away in 1830. King Leopold II established a private company to exploit the Congo during the late nineteenth century, which was renamed the Belgian Congo in 1908. It also gained what is now Rwanda and Burundi after World War I. Belgium was occupied by Germany during both World Wars. It was a founder member of the EEC (now the EU).

Speaking

In Belgium there are three linguistic groups (French, Dutch, and German) and ten provinces (Hainaut, Namur, Liège, Walloon Brabant, Luxembourg, West Flanders, East Flanders, Flemish Brabant, Antwerp, and Limburg).

Try to be aware of whom you are addressing and to which group they belong (asking "Where are you from?" is always a good idea). Avoid discussing personal matters or linguistic divisions with Belgians. Don't compare the

Flemish with the Dutch or the Walloons with the French. Safe topics of conversation on first meeting include the weather, traffic, the family, and work.

Belgians respect other cultures and dislike people who express strong opinions. Boasting and showing off are not welcome and will elicit a swift change of subject. Don't be too assertive or try to pull rank.

Use Monsieur, Madame, or Mademoiselle for French-speakers, or Meneer, Mevrouw, or Juffrouw for Flemish-speakers, to mean Mr., Mrs., or Miss.

Speak in a calm and composed manner at all times; raising your voice in public or using animated gestures is unwelcome. If you feel angry, trying to resolve a conflict with calm politeness and tact yields the best results.

Belgians are private, so asking, "What do you do?" to a stranger is considered intrusive and rude. It would be more tactful to bring your own occupation into the conversation; this way the other person can discuss his or her profession should they choose.

Body language

Belgians are not very tactile, so allow at least an arm's length of personal space and avoid overt physical expressions, such as hugging

and backslapping, unless you know someone very well.

Belgian friends of both sexes touch alternate cheeks and air kiss to greet and say goodbye.

During mealtimes keep your hands on the table, not in your lap. It is polite to wait until all members of your party are seated and have been served before eating. Don't start drinking until the toast has been made. Glasses are raised twice during a toast; once during the verbal toast and then after exchanging glances.

In Belgium, it is customary for men to stand up when a woman enters the room. Foreign men should take their lead from the other men in the room as to when they should sit down again.

Talking to someone with your hands in your pockets, snapping your fingers, or pointing with your index finger is considered very rude.

Sense of humor

Belgians have a subtle and self-deprecating sense of humor which can also be absurdist and subversive. For example, they are very fond of one of their most famous tourist attractions—the Manneken Pis in Brussels—a tiny statue of a little boy urinating in a fountain.

Brazil

National character

Brazilians are very optimistic and resourceful people who have a concept called jeito which means that there is always a solution to every problem—even if it means bending the rules or employing a little well-placed nepotism. They are gregarious and welcoming, and while they by no means bottle up their emotions, they tend to be more analytical than other Latin Americans. Collectively, Brazilians are well known for being very friendly and social.

The country is predominantly Roman Catholic and loyalty to family is more important in Brazil than in any other Latin American country. There is a large ethnic mix, too. For example, the country has the largest number of Japanese people outside of Japan, and German is the second most spoken language after Portuguese.

The culture is very gregarious and risk-oriented, but promptness is a low priority. It is not unusual for a Brazilian to be fifteen minutes late to a business appointment or meeting with friends.

A brief history

Before the arrival of Portuguese explorers, Brazil had been home to many semi-nomadic tribes for ten thousand years. But then the Portuguese exploited the country for its mineral wealth, sugar cane, and coffee beans. Soon after, hundreds of thousands of slaves were imported from Africa to work on plantations. There was another huge influx of people after gold was newly discovered by the Portuguese soon after their settlement of the coast in the 16th century.

When Napoleon occupied Portugal in 1807, the Portuguese royal family—Queen Maria I of Portugal and her son, the future John VI of Portugal—fled to Rio de Janeiro, along with the government and the rest of the aristocrats. During this time Brazil briefly acted as the center of the Portuguese empire. On December 16, 1815, John raised Brazil to the status of a kingdom. He returned to Portugal in 1822 and a brief war ensued, but Brazil was able to declare its independence on September 7 of that year. This independence was recognized in a formal treaty with Britain and Portugal on August 29, 1825.

Slavery was abolished in 1888 and then, in the late nineteenth century, Brazil started to become industrialized. During this time coffee replaced sugar as the country's major export. Soon after, King Pedro II was overthrown by the military on November 15, 1889, and Brazil became a federal republic. Another wave of immigration saw more than five million European, Arab, and Japanese incomers. During the twentieth century Brazil's rubber industry boomed, until its monopoly was broken when a rival industry was established in 1910 in East Asia by the British East India Company using seeds stolen from Brazil. The country also experienced three dictatorships (1930 to 1934, 1937 to 1945, and 1964 to 1985). Today, Brazil is a multiparty federal republic with a president and free elections.

Speaking

Portuguese is Brazil's official language, although there are enclaves of French, German, and Italian speakers. Brazil is the only Portuguese-speaking nation in the Americas, and Brazilians do not consider themselves to be Hispanic. Note that they do not like to be addressed in Spanish. They do not like being referred to as "Latins," either.

Conversations can get quite loud and animated with much gesturing.

Say "Oi" for "Hi" and "Ciao" for "Bye."

Brazilians are expressive and passionate conversationalists. Soccer, family, and children are always popular topics. Be prepared to interrupt and be interrupted—it's not rude, just an indication of how enthusiastically Brazilians throw themselves into conversation.

Body language

Brazilians are very tactile; physical contact is an important part of communication, so expect plenty of it—especially touching of arms, elbows, and backs. A first meeting will involve a handshake with good eye contact, but men often hug and backslap friends and women tend to exchange cheek to cheek air kisses as they shake hands. Men shake hands with women, and exchange air kisses with established female friends and family.

Personal space is very small, so don't back away if a Brazilian stands too close to you.

Flicking your finger underneath your chin means "I don't know" or "I don't understand." Wiping your hands together means "It doesn't matter."

Avoid using the OK sign and the thumbs up gesture, both of which are considered rude (sexual).

Sense of humor

During a state visit to Brazil, French president Charles DeGaulle is reputed to have remarked, "Ce n'est pas un pays sérieux" (This is not a serious country). Comedy appears to be endemic in Brazilian society. The Brazilian sense of humor is based on making fun of everything from Portuguese immigrants to corrupt politicians. (Manuel, a Portuguese immigrant living in Brazil phones the airport and asks, "How long does it take to fly to Lisbon?" The clerk replies "Just a minute . . ." so Manuel thanks her and hangs up.) The quality of ludus (playfulness) is greatly valued.

Bulgaria

National character

Of Bulgaria's eight million people, about 85 percent are of Slavic ancestry and 10 percent are of Turkish ancestry. Other minority groups make up the last 5 percent. They include Armenians, Greeks, Gypsies, Romanians, and Russians. About two-thirds of all Bulgarians live in urban areas. They are a fun loving and gregarious people who pride themselves on their hospitality and neighborliness. They are well-educated, hardworking, and very proud of their culture and heritage, but they are modest and do not respond well to those who try to pull status or show off about their achievements. The family is very important: many generations may live under one roof and deference is shown towards elders. About two-thirds of all Bulgarians live in urban areas, and space can be cramped with large families, although living conditions have improved greatly since 1990.

A brief history

The area that is now Bulgaria has been occupied for thousands of years. The Thracians (various ancient peoples who spoke Dacian and Thracian) arrived around 3000 B.C. The history of Bulgaria as a separate country began in the seventh century with the arrival of the Bulgars. During the time of the late Roman Empire, the area was split into several provinces: Dacia, Dardania, Hemimont, Macedonia, Moesia, Rhodope, Scythia, and Thrace. During the sixth and seventh centuries there was an influx of Slavic tribes, including the Bulgars. These tribes united to defeat the Byzantines to form the first Bulgarian State in 681 A.D., which grew in size and strength until it became the center of Slavonic culture. The Cyrillic alphabet was devised in Bulgaria and was only later used by the Russians.

In 1018 Bulgaria became a Byzantine province. The second Bulgarian state was proclaimed after a revolution in 1185. In the fourteenth century the country was overrun by the Turks to become the province of Roumelia in the Ottoman Empire. An independence movement developed during the nineteenth century, leading to Russia declaring war on the Ottoman Empire and liberating Bulgaria. During the First and Second Balkan Wars of 1912 and 1913, Bulgaria, Serbia, and Greece drove the Turks out of Eastern Roumelia. In the ensuing peace Bulgaria had to cede territory including Macedonia. Bulgaria allied with Germany during both World Wars to try to regain this territory. During the Cold War Bulgaria became a satellite of the Soviet Union. After a bloodless revolution in 1989 the first democratic elections took place. Bulgaria joined the European Union in January 2007.

Speaking

The official language is Bulgarian, however English is widely used. German is also spoken and a number of people in the capital, Sofia, have knowledge of French as well.

Be aware that relations between Bulgaria and Turkey have historically always been strained, as Bulgaria struggled for a long time against Ottoman occupation. So don't bring up the subject of Turkey.

Body language

Bulgarians, especially the older generation, shake their heads to say "Yes" and nod to say "No."

Initial greetings are quite formal and reserved. The most common greeting is a firm handshake with good eye contact. Close friends hug and kiss on the cheek. It is polite to greet the oldest in the group first.

Wedding bands are worn on the ring finger of the right hand.

Making a toast when drinking liquor is expected. Raise your glass and lightly clink with those of everyone else

while looking them in the eye and saying, "Naz drave" (Good health).

On the street or in other public places, strangers usually avoid making eye contact. On public transportation it is customary for young people to give up their seats to older women or to parents with young children. There is a well organized public transport system in the cities and in many smaller towns. There are buses, trolleys (in many cities), and trams in Sofia, which also has a small metro system.

Sense of humor

Bulgaria has a strong oral tradition of tales, songs, sayings, jokes, riddles, spells, and curses that show wit and often a dark humor. The Bulgarian sense of humor coincides with the American sense of humor (only some would say they are even friendlier). The town of Gabrovo is considered the Bulgarian humor capital, and is the target of jokes about thriftiness and stinginess. The town's symbol is a black cat without a tail—the joke being that the town's residents cut the tails off their cats so that when they let the cats out they can close the door a fraction earlier to preserve heat.

Canada

National character

Canadians are self-reliant and individualistic, though more reserved and risk-averse than Americans, and their pace of life is rather sedentary. While success is measured by personal achievement, consensus and tolerance towards others is very important. There is some tension between the French province of Quebec (which is very ethnocentric), and the other Canadian provinces. Citizens of Quebec tend to be more private and reserved.

Canadians are quite logical thinkers who can look at problems objectively; rules and facts hold sway over subjective feelings. They have a cultural identity that is distinct from that of the U.S. and object to being lumped together with their southern neighbor. Thanks in part to the transcontinental railroad, completed in 1885, Canada enjoys cultural diversity across its nation—not just in major metropolitan cities. They are proud of their cultural icons (the flag, moose, beer, the beaver, Mounties, Shania Twain, ice hockey, maple syrup, etc.) but resist being defined by them.

A brief history

The first inhabitants of Canada were the Inuit and the people of the First Nations (Native Americans). The French set up the first European colony in 1534 in what is now Quebec, and the British arrived about fifty years later to colonize Newfoundland. After the Seven Years War, the French army abandoned its colony and Quebec became a British interest. The British colonies in Canada didn't break away like those in America, because generally they were given greater autonomy, and many loyalist U.S. citizens moved there. The colonies were unified on July 1, 1867, under the British North America Act. This date is seen as the origin of Canada as a country, although at this stage it was still called the Dominion of Canada.

Canada expanded its frontier west, but without the violence and lawlessness seen in the American Wild West. In 1931 Canada gained independence from Great Britain, and since 1949 it has been known as the Canadian Confederation with a federal multiparty parliamentary democracy. The British monarch acts as the nominal head of state.

Speaking

Canada is a bilingual country with two official languages: English and French. Quebec is mainly French-speaking and the rest of Canada is broadly English-speaking—however, New Brunswick is very mixed. Chinese and Italian are the next most common languages.

English-speaking people rarely interrupt someone when they are speaking, but

French-speakers are more flexible, and will often cut in.

Body language

In business and in formal situations, greet using a firm handshake and with good eye contact. In more informal circumstances it is acceptable to raise your hand, or do a group wave, and say "Hi." Men should wait for a woman to extend her hand for a handshake. The French shake hands more frequently (at several encounters with the same person during a single day) and continental cheek-kissing is common among French-speakers, who are generally more animated, use more gestures, and are tactile. Overall, they have smaller personal space than English speakers.

Speak in a calm manner. Canadians are straight talkers who expect honesty. Hyperbole and hype will be viewed with distrust.

Try to use open body language that exposes the heart and is welcoming, but avoid vigorous gesturing. Closed gestures such as arm-folding, leg crossing, hand-hiding, and fidgeting will send out subconscious signals that you are standoffish or ill at ease.

Both the thumbs up and the OK sign (forming a circle with the thumb and index finger) are expressions of approval and agreement.

To beckon someone, face the palm upwards and wave your fingers together back and forth.

Backslapping is common among English-speakers, but rarely used by the French-speakers.

It is acceptable to sit casually (except in the most formal of circumstances), such as placing one ankle over your other leg's knee.

Sense of humor

The Canadian sense of humor (Jim Carrey notwithstanding) is dry, with a strong sense of irony and satire. Favorite targets of a joke include politicians and self-parody, such as the pair of fictional Canadian brothers Bob and Doug McKenzie, who played upon Canadian stereotypes on Canadian television in the 1980s. Canada's cultural identity as being separate from the U.S. became the humorous subject of the hugely successful "I am a Canadian" series of Molson beer ads that aired in the 1990s and early 2000s. They featured a man named Joe, an "average Canadian," standing in front of different images relating to Canadian culture, and talking about his differences from Americans.

Chile

than in the other Latin America countries (its first female president was elected in 2006).

National character

Chileans can be a reserved and sometimes quite formal bunch. The extended family is very important, and maintaining one's honor and that of one's family is paramount. Honesty and integrity are highly valued. Chileans have respect for law and order (unlike in some South American countries, the police are trustworthy: bribing them will land you in serious trouble) and are quite conservative when it comes to improvising or taking risks. Equality of the sexes is marginally better

A brief history

The first European settlers arrived from Spain in the early sixteenth century. Spain became part of the Spanish Empire until independence was achieved on February 12, 1818, led by Bernado O'Higgins and with Argentine support. Expansion followed in the nineteenth century, as Chile fought Peru and Bolivia for control of the coastline. As a result, Bolivia is now a landlocked country, and there is still tension between the two nations.

Marxist leader Salvador Allende won the presidency in 1970 but was overthrown by the military and the Central Intelligence Agency in 1973. General Augusto Pinochet became president and his repressive regime lasted until free elections were held in 1989, when he lost power. Today Chile is a multiparty republic with free elections, but there is still major inequality and poverty in the country.

Speaking

The official language is Spanish, but English is widely spoken in the business community.

It is acceptable to interrupt others while they are speaking, rather than follow the more linear approach of taking turns. There may also be two or three topics of conversation on the go at the same time within a group. If you are interrupted take it as a sign that people are engaged in the conversation, rather than take offense.

Chileans are honest and straightforward, but their desire to accommodate often leads them to give a non-committal or diplomatic reply, rather than the plain truth. For example, if a Chilean wanted to make a criticism he would rather give a long-winded speech that reveals his concerns gradually, rather than come straight to the point.

Chileans dislike confrontation and will always try to find a path that shows kindness and

respect for others. Don't lose your temper or raise your voice, as you will only lose respect; don't openly single out someone for criticism.

Avoid talking about local politics, religion, and human rights violations. Good topics of conversation include family, cuisine (such as empanada, humitas, cazuela de ave, bife lo probe), wines (Chile produces some fabulous Cabernet Sauvignons, Merlots, Pinot Noirs, Chardonnays, and Sauvignon Blancs, and Maipo Valley is its most famous wine valley), and local sights of interest (from Santiago's urban attractions to the spectacular beauty of the Andes, the bubbling mud fields of the El Tatio Geysers or the alien landscape of Moon Valley).

Body language
Even though South American countries have a reputation for being laid-back, it is important to maintain good posture, and keep your hands out of your pockets. Do not yawn or stretch in public. Men should stand when a woman enters the room.

Initial greetings are quite formal, with handshakes and direct eye contact. Chileans are reserved until they get to know you better, although they will warm up quickly. Greet the eldest person first. Close male friends may hug and backslap, and women usually kiss the air once above the right cheek.

Personal space is small. Chileans stand close, so don't back away. If you do, they may think you are being shy or standoffish, and will quickly close the gap again.

When toasting, say "Salut!" (Health) while maintaining eye contact.

Slapping your right fist in your left open palm is considered obscene.

Chileans are heavy smokers. Always offer everyone a cigarette before lighting up.

Sense of humor
Chilean humor is quite dry and ironic and can be difficult for an outsider to understand. Chileans will often punctuate a joke by laughing, so follow their cue, and you will recognize not to take them literally or be confused.

One of the most famous vehicles of Chilean humor is the comic strip Condorito, a condor fitted in black soccer shorts, a red shirt, beret, and flip-flops. It was created over fifty years ago by Rene Rios Boettiger, who is widely known as Pepo.

China

National character

China is a relationship-driven culture, where family, "face" (personal standing among one's peers), and etiquette are of vital importance. The Chinese are extremely efficient and hard workers. The society is very hierarchical and great respect is shown towards the elderly. Humility and modesty are also considered desirable traits. Punctuality is very important. The Chinese are very superstitious: before important decisions are made, such as the conclusion of a business deal, they will consider whether it is an auspicious time or day.

A brief history

China is one of the oldest civilizations in the world, and its recorded history dates back more than 4,000 years. The first Chinese ruling dynasty was the Hsia, around 2200 B.C. The final dynasty, the Ch'ing, ended in 1911, after which the Republic of China was founded by Sun Yat-sen. The country became Communist in 1949, after Mao Tse-tung took control, and decades of disastrous policies followed, during which hundreds of thousands of dissidents were executed and imprisoned and many millions starved to death. Since the much publicized massacre of protestors in Tiananmen Square in 1989, China has been increasingly under world scrutiny about its human rights abuses. However, its unprecedented economic growth, and its hardworking population of over one billion people, means that it is set to become the superpower of the twenty-first century.

Speaking

A common greeting is "Have you eaten?" to which you should reply, "Yes, thank you," even if you haven't.

The Chinese are very diplomatic and are reluctant to say "No," instead often saying something like "Perhaps," or "I'll consider it." Saving face is very important in China, so people are ever keen to avoid situations of potential embarrassment. By contrast, they do not say "Thank you" ("Shee shee") very often, preferring to save it for truly significant expressions of gratitude.

The family is very important in China, but you should refrain from asking people whether they are married, as it can be a sensitive subject. However, Chinese people are very flattered when you show an interest in their children, or ask about the health of their parents (taking care of one's parents is a virtue).

Personal relationships may take time to develop. As a sign of respect Chinese people may be reluctant to use your first name, preferring instead to call your "Mr." "Mrs.," or "Miss," plus your surname, or your title if you have one (e.g. Doctor). Once they do use your given name, you can be sure that they feel relaxed with you.

In Chinese the surname comes first followed by the given name or names, so a name like "Thomas Jefferson" would be "Jefferson Thomas."

Compliments will be deflected with a modest comment such as "It was nothing," rather than the more direct "Thank you" common in West-

31

ern cultures. Likewise, when you are thanking someone, don't make too big a deal of it, as you will cause embarrassment.

Body language
The standard form of greeting is a bow from the shoulder or a nod of the head, often without smiling, but as a foreigner you can also expect to shake hands, but don't expect a bone-crusher, or grip too hard yourself. Always stand up when being introduced and remain standing throughout the introductions.

Greetings can be a quite formal and solemn affair. Avoiding eye contact used to be customary in China, but this has changed greatly, especially among the younger generation.

Although the Chinese are courteous people, this does not extend to waiting in lines. You can expect to be pushed and shoved.

Keep gestures to a minimum. Chinese people use them infrequently, and may find them irritating and confusing. Avoid backslapping and other tactile gestures such as putting an arm around someone's shoulder or hugging. However, expect to see same sex friends of both sexes holding hands while walking down the street.

Public displays of emotion aren't acceptable but they are unavoidable in the hustle and bustle of this high populous country.

Maintain the same personal space as you would in Western society, but if a Chinese person comes closer, do not back away.

Chinese people routinely spit on the floor. They believe that mucus is poisonous and should not be swallowed. However the government has tried to discourage this practice as it offends tourists.

Don't point with an index finger: use an open hand instead. Don't snap your fingers, whistle, or show the soles of your feet.

Sense of humor
Laughter and smiling is often the result of nervousness or miscomprehension. Irony and sarcasm are not generally recognized in China. If you are being sarcastic or wry, you will need to exaggerate it, since subtle attempts at irony will be misunderstood and could cause offense. While part of the pleasure of a Western joke is that the listener makes some of the connections, the Chinese prefer to have their punch lines spelled out for them.

Croatia

National character

Croatians are very hospitable, down to earth and direct, and they have suffered a great deal to achieve the independence they have today. They are a confident, outgoing, independent, internationalist and forward-looking people who do not like to discuss their personal tragedies and problems. The main social unit is the family, with many people living in extended family units. Croatia's population weighs in at 4.5 million people.

A brief history

The area known today as Croatia has been populated since the Stone Age. During early recorded history its inhabitants included the Illyrians, Celts, and the Greeks. In the seventh century Croatia was organized into two dukedoms: Pannonian Croatia in the north and Littoral Croatia in the south; these were united in 925 by King Tomislav. At the end of the twelfth century Croatia fell under the rule of Hungary and feudalism was introduced, and later the country lost a lot of territory to the Ottoman Empire. During the sixteenth century the Austro-Hungarian Habsburg Monarchy took control and by the 1700s they had driven the Ottomans out.

Before the end of World War I, Croatia broke away from Austria-Hungary and became part of the State of Slovenes. In 1929, King Aleksandar proclaimed a dictatorship and Croatia became part of the newly-named Yugoslavia. The fascist Ustaše Party took control during World War II, forming the "Independent State of Croatia," and killed over 200,000 of its ethnic minorities. After the war Croatia became part of the communist Social Federal Republic of Yugoslavia, under Tito, and the country recovered economically, through industrialization and tourism. After Tito's death, ethnic difficulties resurfaced, leading to the Croatian War of Independence (1991 to 1995). Since the end of that war the country is a safe place for tourists, with a very low crime rate. Today it is still recovering from its war wounds and has started the process of joining the European Union.

Speaking

A common greeting is "Zdravo," which means "Hello," or "Bog," which means "God" and is used for both "Hi" and "Bye." Shake hands firmly and maintain good eye contact.

Avoid talking about the recent war or comparing Croats and Serbians.

Good topics of conversation include Mediterranean cuisine, food and cooking, and wine. Croatians are switched on to world events and they are passionate about many sports, including soccer, tennis, rugby, basketball, and water polo.

Body language

The customary greeting between both men and women is a firm handshake. Closer friends will give each other a kiss on each cheek.

Men are not very tactile, so you should avoid close physical contact such as back slapping, or putting an arm around the shoulder, until you know someone very well and can judge their comfort level.

Croatians use their arms and hands a great deal while speaking, especially in the costal regions.

It is important to maintain regular eye contact; otherwise you will be viewed as untrustworthy, disinterested, or insecure.

Never raise your thumb, index, and middle fingers at once. This is a Serbian gesture and is connected to Serbian nationalism. If you want to indicate the number three, use different fingers.

Croatians are direct communicators, who often leave the responsibility on the other person with regard to accepting or refusing an invitation. For example, a Croat may announce that he will drop by to see you that evening, on the assumption that if you are unable to or don't want to meet, that you will be direct enough to say so. No offense will be taken.

Speak loudly enough for people to hear you. People who speak softly are seen as lacking in self-confidence.

Sense of humor

Croatians enjoy irony, cynicism, and dark humor. A joke may be delivered without any facial cues such as a wink or a smile, so be alert to deadpan delivery. Anyone can be the target of a joke, so learn to laugh at yourself, as you could be the next victim. Croatians love to pull your leg, especially if you are a newcomer; take it as a sign of acceptance and a desire to make a connection with you.

The Czech Republic

National character

The Czechs are a modest, egalitarian, peaceful, and fun-loving people, who appear reserved until you get to know them well. They are well-educated with a literacy rate of 99 percent. Academic achievements and titles are esteemed, but it is not acceptable to brag about them. Knowledge and ability are ranked above status, and external shows of wealth, such as ostentatiously expensive clothing, are rarely exhibited (except among the younger generation). Due to lack of space and financial limitations, many members of the same family may live under the same roof, but the family remains an important social unit and great respect is shown towards the elderly.

A brief history

In the Iron Age, the area known today as the Czech Republic was occupied by Celtic Boii tribes, who had wanted to flee the Romans. Slavic tribes have occupied the country since the fifth century A.D. and formed into two groups: the Czechs in the west, and the Slovaks in the east. In 900 A.D. the Slovaks were conquered by the Hungarian Magyar tribe, while Prague in the west became the seat of the Holy Roman Empire. During the Middle Ages the region was a center for the Protestant Reformation. During the seventeenth century the whole country fell under the control of the Austro-Hungarian Habsburg dynasty. The independent state of Czechoslovakia was formed after the break up of the Habsburg Empire at the end of World War I.

The country was again occupied by the Nazis during World War II. It was liberated by the Russians and became a Soviet satellite for the next forty years. In 1989 the peaceful "Velvet Revolution" brought democracy, and the election of the dissident writer, Václav Havel, as president. In 1993, again peacefully, the country divided into the Czech and Slovak republics in what became known as the "Velvet Divorce." Today the Czech Republic is a multiparty parliamentary democracy, with a president as head of state and a prime minister as head of government.

Speaking

The official language is Czech, a West Slavic language related to Polish, but Russian, English, and German are also spoken with varying degrees of fluency.

Czech is a difficult language to learn, but any attempts to speak it will be welcomed and help to make a good impression. At first meeting Czechs may often appear reserved and guarded, but as long as you are direct and approachable they will quickly loosen up, although close friendships are formed very slowly. Avoid using first names until you are invited to do so. The use of first names is confined to older family members addressing younger ones and to close friends. It can take a long time to move a relationship onto a first-name basis. Young people will move quickly to first name terms, but in business and among the older generation, people prefer to be called by their title or surname.

While it is true that post-Communism successful businesspeople now have visible wealth, Czechs are generally very egalitarian, so avoid showing off your status or pulling rank. Compliments are likely to be modestly deflected rather than accepted with a "Thank you."

Speak clearly and maintain good eye contact to show attentiveness and trustworthiness. Czech people are quite loud and expressive, while maintaining formality and correctness.

Good topics of conversation include Czech beer, sports (especially soccer, ice hockey, and cycling), music, and dogs.

Czechs are well-informed about politics, and are happy to voice their opinions. Be careful to avoid criticism of either Czechs or Slovaks—or the former Communist regime.

Body language

Czechs are warm and welcoming, but their introductions can be quite formal. Use a firm handshake with good eye contact. Wait for a woman or elderly person to extend their hand. Cheek kissing is quite rare. However, public displays of affection between friends and lovers are common.

Gestures are minimal, and there is little tolerance for speakers who gesture a lot; they tend to find it distracting and ill-mannered. It you see someone moving their head from the right to the left, while frowning, watch what you are saying or minimize your gestures.

Czechs don't smile at people they don't know, so if you happen to catch someone's eye in public your smile of acknowledgement will be met with surprise.

Rude gestures to avoid include waving a lifted fist or a pointed index finger. You should avoid pointing in general.

Czechs always take off their shoes when entering someone's home.

Sense of humor

Czech humor is overt and blunt, often quite black, dirty, and politically incorrect (and may include racial slurs). For example, the director of civilian counter-intelligence recently joked to reporters about the Czech's response to terrorism: "When there is a bomb attack at a seaside resort, other foreigners do not visit the location for some time. On the contrary, Czechs go to this particular site because the prices of the stays fall."

Denmark

National character

Danes are proud and egalitarian people who value tolerance, diversity, and gender equality. Its homogenous population is well-educated. As with the rest of Scandinavia, the people seek to minimize social difference with high taxes to provide a strong welfare state, and feel a responsibility to help those who are less fortunate. Social categories are defined by education and occupation rather than income groups. Well-off Danes do not flaunt their wealth; displays of material superiority are discouraged, and for this reason informality is considered a virtue.

Danes are not rule-oriented; in fact they are very adept at finding a way to bend the rules to find solutions. Families, while generally small, are still the emotional and cultural hub of the social structure. The flag—a horizontal white cross on a red field—symbolizes a membership community and a sense of inclusion. Only 15 percent of the population lives in rural areas, and many of those people work in cities.

A brief history

Denmark has been continually inhabited since the last ice age, with much Celtic influence, and it avoided invasion by the Roman Empire. The Vikings inhabited Denmark between the eighth and eleventh centuries, and conducted raids throughout Europe. In the tenth century A.D. Harold Bluetooth established the unified kingdom of Denmark and converted to Christianity, which replaced the old Norse mythology.

Denmark was briefly united with England under King Canute during the early eleventh century and was rocked by civil wars during the twelfth century, but it grew into a major power in the Baltic Sea under Valdemar the Great. In 1387, Denmark—which already ruled Norway, Iceland, and the Faroe Islands—acquired Sweden under the Union of Kalmar and was ruled by Danish Queen Margaret I, who was married to the king of Norway. The Union disintegrated into civil war under her successor, Eric of Pomerania.

The Lutheran Church was introduced in 1536 and Denmark quickly became the heartland of Lutheranism. In the mid-seventeenth century Denmark lost a war with Sweden and relinquished three of its richest provinces. In the eighteenth century Denmark colonized Greenland. In 1814 Denmark (by now bankrupt) gave Norway to Sweden under the Treaty of Kiel as punishment for giving its support to Napoleon during the Napoleonic Wars (Norway revolted soon afterwards). Denmark became a constitutional monarchy in 1849. It was invaded by the Nazis during World War II and was a founding member of both NATO and the EEC (now the EU). Today

it is a constitutional monarchy, with a prime minister as the head of government.

Speaking

The official language is Danish, spoken by 98 percent of the population, although many Danes also speak German and English. Danes are direct speakers, but they are reserved with strangers, and are reluctant to make small talk with them.

Speak in a moderate voice, and avoid any behavior which draws attention to yourself. Don't call across the street to greet a friend.

Danes tend not to use the greeting "How are you?" rhetorically, as people do in the U.S.

Don't lump Danes in with the other Scandinavian cultures; be sensitive to the country's uniqueness.

An overt display of public emotion is considered a sign of weakness. Danes seek to avoid confrontation, and they dislike being interrupted while they are speaking.

Body language

First meeting is by handshake with everyone present—women first and including children—while maintaining good eye contact and smiling. Danes usually introduce themselves by their first names.

Complimenting someone's physical appearance (such as clothes) doesn't sit comfortably in Denmark. Such compliments are considered too intimate and are inappropriate, although it is acceptable to pass favorable comments that are non-personal (such as admiring someone's house, cooking, or a job well done).

Danes are modest and reserved until you get to know them better; they do not gesture much and are not very tactile, so avoid exaggerated gestures, back slapping, arm touching, or hugging unless you know someone and their preferences well. Personal space is wide.

Danes are very polite and say "Thank you" a lot.

Sense of humor

Danish humor is full of irony, so someone making a joke may mean the opposite of what they say. For example, saying "Great weather" may be an ironic observation that it has just started raining.

Egypt

National character

Egypt enjoys a relatively homogeneous population, of which the overwhelming majority (over 90 percent) is Arabic-speaking Sunni Muslims. Most of the remainder is Coptic Christians. Despite this, it is one of the most westernized nations in the Middle East. The family unit is very important, and Egyptians are very friendly and hospitable. However there is an enormous gap between rich and poor, and the culture reinforces the concept that wealth equates to status, self-worth, and importance. One-third of the population is below a poverty line set by the Egyptian government.

While Egyptians are very friendly and welcoming, a visitor to Egypt needs to be patient with the pace of life. Bureaucracy is notorious, and meetings and appointments rarely occur on time and face constant interruptions.

A brief history

Major civilizations have occupied Egypt for the last 7,000 years. After the Pharaonic and Greco-Roman periods, Egypt became Christian, until it was conquered my Muslims in the seventh century A.D. It became part of the Ottoman Empire in the sixteenth century, and

at the end of the eighteenth century it was conquered by Napoleon. The English drove out the French in 1801, then the Ottomans ruled until English occupation in 1882. The Suez Canal was completed in 1869, linking the Mediterranean to the Red Sea. Britain occupied the country in 1882, and after World War I Egyptian nationalism grew. During World War II, part of Egypt was invaded by Germany and Italy, but the Allies gained a decisive victory at El Alamein in 1942.

In 1952, a revolution forced King Farouk to abdicate and Egypt became a republic. Gamal al-Nasir (Nasser) became president in 1954. Egypt was defeated in 1967 by Israel in the Six-Day War, which started because Egypt had closed the Suez Canal. Israel destroyed the Egyptian Air Force and occupied Sinai. Nasser died in 1970, and his successor Anwar al-Sadat launched an unsuccessful attack on Israel in 1973. Menachem Begin, then Israel's leader, surprised the world by signing a historic peace treaty in 1979. Sadat was assassinated by opponents in 1981, and was succeeded by his vice president, Hosni Mubarak.

Speaking

The official language is Arabic but English is the most common foreign language spoken. Many Egyptians are fluent in French as well.

The traditional Arab greeting involves repeated expressions of welcome, with questions about health, family and often invoking God's favor ("Insha' Allah" which means "If it is God's will"). Two Arab men will take each other's right hands, placing their left hand on the other's shoulder and kissing each cheek. More Westernized men use a simple handshake. Kissing should only take place between members of the same sex, and you should only shake hands with a woman if she extends her hand.

Greetings should precede all forms of social interaction. If you join a group, even of strangers, you should greet everyone present.

Don't bring up the subject of other people's wives and daughters. If you visit an Egyptian's house, his wife will probably be in the kitchen, but don't mention or acknowledge her unless your host does, or unless she speaks to you. Don't be too complimentary about any household items, since your host may feel obliged to give them to you.

Sport is a safe topic, including soccer, boxing, basketball, and horseracing. A good conversational icebreaker is your positive experience of Egypt. Avoid talking about politics or religion.

Public display of anger is discouraged; always be polite and respectful.

Egyptians are great lovers of language and debate. You are encouraged to express and back up your opinions; speech is full of poetical language and hyperbole. "Yes" often means "Maybe."

Do not look women in the eye and do not talk to members of the opposite sex who are strangers; it will be interpreted as a sexual advance.

Body language

Personal space is very close; don't back away even if you feel that your personal space is being invaded, as this will be interpreted as rejection. Expect a lot of physical contact. Egyptians shake hands very often during a conversation as a sign of friendship and unity.

Eat and pass plates of food with your right hand. (The left hand is reserved for unclean uses, such as going to the bathroom.)

Male friends often hold hands while walking together, as do female friends. However, public displays of affection between the opposite sexes are unacceptable.

Don't show the bottom of your feet and don't cross your legs when sitting.

The thumbs-up gesture is rude, and so is pointing: use the open hand. Tapping two index fingers together means a couple are sleeping together, or can mean "Do you want to sleep together?"

Touching all the fingers together and bobbing the hand up and down in front of you in a weighing motion, with the palm facing inwards, means "Calm down" or "Wait a moment."

Sense of humor

Egyptian humor is often self-deprecating, but don't join in and start insulting someone (or the country) with western banter.

Finland

National character

Finnish people are straightforward, hard-working, and stubborn; these characteristics are popularly referred to with the Finnish term "Sisu." The culture is also egalitarian, individualistic, and liberal. Finland is a remarkably homogenous country with a broad political consensus. Ostentatious behaviors—such as boasting or visible displays of wealth—are unwelcome, since the Finns tend to be rather quiet, even private and withdrawn. They are great lovers of the outdoors, and a sporting tradition is engrained from birth in boys and girls. Drinking and relaxing in saunas are two favorite activities of Finnish people.

A brief history

The area that is now Finland has been inhabited for about ten thousand years. Its history has always been closely entwined with that of Sweden, and it fell under Swedish control in the twelfth century. Originally the name "Finland" referred to a small area in the southwest—the country as we know it today was unified by the effects of the Catholic Church, which was brought to Finland by Swedish settlers.

In 1550 the future capital, Helsinki, was founded by Gustav Vasa, the King of Sweden. However, it remained little more than a small fishing village for the next 200 years. In the seventeenth century Sweden and Finland fought together against Protestantism in the Thirty Years' War. At the end of the century a famine killed about 30 percent of the population, and a few years later Finland was occupied by Russia. In 1809 it became the autonomous Grand Duchy of Finland.

During the nineteenth century the Finnish desire for a cultural identity separate from its neighbors grew, and was expressed by the popular credo, "We are not Swedes, and we do not wish to become Russian, so let us be Finns." It finally declared its independence in 1917. During World War II, Finland fought the Soviet Union twice, and had to pay enormous reparations after the war. During the Cold War Finland's politics were influenced by the Soviet Union but the country never became a satellite state. It joined the European Union in 1995.

Speaking

Finland has two official languages: Finnish and Swedish, but English is widely spoken. Finns are proud of their country and expect you to know a little about it even though they may be culturally insular themselves (at the very least, you should know that the mobile phone company Nokia is Finnish, not Japanese). It is worth brushing up on some Finnish achievements before you visit. For example, Finnish glassware and Arabia pottery, Marimekko fabrics and modern furniture, and Finnish modern architecture are all famous around the world. Finland is also well-respected for its musical talent: Jean Sibelius was one of the most notable composers of the late nineteenth and early twentieth centuries.

Small talk is not an important part of Finnish communication. They are straight talkers who like to consider what they are saying, and they are not afraid to pause for extended periods of time to reflect or gather their thoughts. It isn't necessary to keep the conversation flowing smoothly; silence is an important part of communication. Be a good listener and don't interrupt. The Finns don't readily talk to strangers on the street, but they will be helpful if approached.

Directness and honesty are important, so don't make promises or extend invitations unless you intend to follow them through. Comments such as "We must do this again sometime" will be taken at face value.

Body language
The standard greeting is a firm handshake with good eye contact. Good friends will embrace, but otherwise Finns rarely embrace or kiss cheeks and are generally not very tactile.

Keep a relaxed and open body language and maintain good eye contact: don't fold your arms, as this may be considered confrontational.

Sense of humor
The Finnish sense of humor is dry, subtle, and witty and often based on double meanings inherent in the language. It may often be delivered with a straight face, in business as well as in casual conversation. However, Finnish comedies are usually slapstick.

France

National character

From a distance, the French national character appears understated and quite reserved. The French tendencies toward rationalism, abstraction, and codification are apparent in all areas of social life. The French respond best to logic and reason over emotion and sentimentality. French bureaucracy is legendary: the systems in France show that every decision is carefully studied before being taken, and that a lot of people have to see the project and give their opinion. That makes the hierarchy very important.

French culture encourages people to express unhappiness and criticize. Protest is a vital part of the French psyche, possibly because ever since the French Revolution, it has worked. France has a reputation as a conservative and reform-resistant nation.

A brief history

Two thousand years ago the Romans conquered the native Celts (the Gauls) and France became part of the Roman Empire for nearly 500 years, until it was ended by a wave of barbaric invasions (from Visigoths, Franks, and Vandals).

The Franks converted to Catholicism and in 800 A.D. Charlemagne, the king of the Franks who had unified France, was crowned the Holy Roman Emperor. Only the Celts in Brittany in the north did not join in this unification and this region of modern-day France retains a distinct Celtic identity.

In 1429 a young peasant, Joan of Arc, rallied the French troops to victory over the English, with whom France had been at war since 1337.

In the seventeenth century King Louis XIV (the "Sun King") captured or bought the land to establish France's borders as they are known today. After his death in 1715 social tension fomented until in 1789 the French Revolution ended the royal dynasty and established a republic. The revolutionary National Assembly divided the country into eighty-three provinces, to replace the previous feudal structure. Ten years later Napoleon seized control of France and ruled until his eventual defeat at the Battle of Waterloo in 1815.

France lost 10 percent of its men and nearly half its industry during World War I; during World War II it surrendered to Germany.

Speaking

Always try to speak the language. If you address a French person in English, their nationalistic pride will make them reluctant to speak in English. However, if you attempt to speak their language, they will more readily switch to English, to help you out. The French take great pride in their language, so mispronounced French may also be met with a shrug of apparent miscomprehension.

Don't address anyone using "tu" (the informal and singular form of "you") if you should have used "vous" (which is used when talking in a respectful manner or to a group of people). If in doubt, use "vous", but beware that if you keep saying "vous" when the other has suggested "tu", it can be seen as unfriendly.

Body language

The ubiquitous cheek kiss (La bise) starts by bringing one cheek close to the other's cheek and simulating a kiss on the cheek. Some start with the right cheek, some with the left. Try to determine which of your cheeks the other is aiming for so an embarrassing collision is avoided. After the first kiss on the cheek, repeat at least once on the opposite cheek. The total number of kisses depends

on the region, the person, and many other things. It may be two, three, and occasionally even four.

The "Gallic shrug" can mean anything from "It's not my fault/responsibility" to "I don't know" or "I disagree." Raise your shoulders and eyebrows, hold your hands in front of you with the palms facing outwards, and pout with your lower lip.

Good posture is very important and a sign of good breeding. Keep your hands out of your pockets and don't slouch.

If someone uses their index finger to pull down the skin under their eye, it means they don't believe what you are saying.

If someone is in trouble, or something is scary or a "close shave," hold up your hand, palm facing your chest, with your fingers loose, and shake it up and down rapidly while saying, "Aïe, aïe, aïe, aïe, aïe!"

When someone makes a loose fist, holds it to their nose, and twists while tilting their head in the other direction they are indicating that someone is drunk: "Il y a un verre dans le nez" (There's a glass in his nose).

To show that you couldn't care less about something, bend your arm toward your shoulder several times, as if you are hitting your shoulder, while saying "Je m'en fous."

Sense of humor

To this day l'humor engagé—political satire and caricature—features prominently in France. Illogical jokes don't work with the French. For example: "The governor of the Bank of England began an address to an assembly of bankers with these words: 'There are three kinds of economists, those who can count and those who can't.'" A joke of this kind would be met with incomprehension by French listeners. It is not logical.

Self-deprecation, another essential ingredient of a "detached" sense of humor, is not the forte of the French. Its two big loves are word play (involving linguistic somersaults that only work in their own language) and farce (they love Jerry Lewis, the American comic they call le roi du crazy; he has even been awarded the Legion of Honor, the country's highest decoration.) Comic films and plays are either farcical or witty, with plenty of wordplays and rapid-fire verbal exchanges.

Germany

National character

There is a strong sense of community and social conscience in German society. Germans are hard working and seek to both do their best while achieving the consensus of those around them. Privacy, punctuality, and respect for one's seniors or superiors are paramount, as well as a deep respect for order and the rule of law. However, there is plenty of room for individual expression, so long as it doesn't break the many rules which govern social behavior, from taking your jacket off in a restaurant (keep it on, even if you are hot) to how you dispose of your rubbish (Germany has a serious and mandatory recycling program which visitors must adhere to). Germans are direct in their speech and their dealings, and value objective facts, logic, and reason above emotion. Their conservative nature means that sudden change is unwelcome.

Many Germans feel a profound affinity with nature and the environment and enjoy experiencing the great outdoors. The roots of this are in German Naturalism that began in the eighteenth century.

A brief history

Germany was originally occupied by numerous tribes, which resisted Roman invasion so that the area east of the Rhine and north of the Danube remained free from Roman occupation. After the fall of the Roman Empire various Germanic tribes were united under Charlemagne in 800 A.D., but the area was soon divided into several regional duchies and principalities which often fought with each other.

In the early Middle Ages a group of trade guilds from more than 200 German towns established the Hanseatic League, which for several centuries maintained a trade monopoly over most of northern Europe. In 1517 Martin Luther started the Protestant reformation when his 95 Theses challenged the Roman Catholic Church. In 1740 Frederick II became ruler of Prussia. Napoleon conquered most of Germany in 1806. The German-speaking kingdoms of Prussia and Austria dominated Europe. Following the fall of Napoleon Bonaparte, the Congress of Vienna convened in 1814 and founded the German Confederation, a loose league of thirty-nine sovereign states. When the state now known as Germany was unified in 1871, Otto von Bismarck became its first Chancellor. He waged war on Denmark, and excluded Austria from the remaining German states.

After World War I Germany became a republic, and the crippling terms of the Versailles Treaty lead to the rise of Hitler's Nazi party and World War II. After that war the country was divided into the Democratic west and the Communist east, until the fall of the Berlin Wall in 1990. Today it is a leading world power and one of the strongest members of the European Union.

Speaking

Germans are direct communicators, and expect others to be honest and straightforward. For example, refusing food is preferable to accepting a second helping out of politeness. Also, praising someone before delivering constructive criticism would be confusing to a German.

Small talk does not play a big part in German interaction. Compliments are not expected and tend to be treated with suspicion.

Eye contact is very important and is held for longer than in many other countries; during conversation it borders on staring.

Always finish your sentences and speak with a clear intention. In some cultures it is common for speakers to trail away at the end of a sentence, but in German the most important part of a sentence often comes at the end. For this reason it is rude to interrupt someone while they are speaking.

German has two forms of "you": one formal ("Sie") and one informal ("du"). If in doubt, use the formal form.

Body language

The personal space is quite wide: about six inches further than hand shaking distance.

Sticking your thumb between your first and second fingers is obscene.

Tapping your index finger on your head indicates that the person to whom you are referring is crazy.

Germans start counting with their thumbs, so if you hold up an index finger it will be interpreted as "two."

Keep your hands out of your pockets and during mealtimes keep them on the table.

The "thumbs up" gesture means is a sign of appreciation or agreement.

Sense of humor

The English language sense of humor often thrives on withholding a vital piece of information until the end of the joke, whereby the final reveal causes a shift of focus which is amusing. However, the sentence structure of the German language is much less flexible, so the "pull back and reveals" and the comedic confusion that arises from double meanings doesn't work in German, where language is much more precise.

Instead of linguistic wordplay, German humor relies more on blunt, seemingly logical and serious statements or observations, which become funny because of their context. For example:

Three priests hold a meeting to discuss where life begins. The evangelical priest says, "No question about it, life begins when the child is born." "No, no," says the Catholic priest, "it all starts when the sperm meets the egg." "You're both wrong," says the Rabbi. "Life begins when the children have left home and the dog is dead."

Germans take business seriously, so joking in a meeting or during a serious negotiation is frowned upon.

Greece

National character

Greeks are hard-working but they also have a laid-back approach to life. Everything in Greece goes slowly and nothing starts on time. Greeks are very people-oriented and tend to make decisions subjectively. Consensus, the family, interpersonal relationships, and absolute loyalty towards your group are very important, and much respect is shown towards the elderly. Greek people are renowned for their hospitality and generosity to foreigners.

A brief history

Greece has a rich and ancient history. The first settlers date from the Paleolithic era (11,000 to 3000 B.C.) and in antiquity Greece saw many great civilizations come and go, including the Minoans and the Mycenaeans. The classic period of ancient Greek history (sixth to fourth centuries B.C.) is credited with the invention of democracy and marked a time of unprecedented intellectual achievement and its great philosophers, politicians, and mathematicians remain world famous.

Since then Greece's history has been a succession of invasions and occupations, by the Macedonian, Roman, Byzantine, and Ottoman empires. Greek independence was hard-won against the Turks during the nineteenth century, when a Greek state was formed in 1831, followed by the establishment of a monarchy. Today Greece is a presidential parliamentary republic.

Speaking

Greeks are infamous for talking loudly in public; they are very friendly and outgoing and will ask many personal questions such as "how much money do you make?" or "why aren't you married?" This is normal and it is OK for you to respond, or deflect the question with a joke, should you choose. Greeks frequently interrupt each other, and talk very openly about themselves. The use of hyperbole and superlatives is common.

Anger may not be expressed directly; it may be expressed by an ironic smile or laugh.

When someone bumps into you in the street, don't take offense if they don't say "Sorry." Hustle and bustle is all part of life. However, generosity and a sense of giving readily are strong, so your "Thank yous" may often be brushed aside as unnecessary.

Body language

Greeks are physically demonstrative and personal space is small. Backing away when you feel that someone is encroaching on your personal space, however, is considered rude. Men hug and kiss each other and even walk arm in arm with relatives and close friends. Friends are greeted with a kiss on both cheeks

Physical gestures are strong and used frequently. Greeks use big gestures with their arms, head, eyes, and lips.

In the older generation "No" is indicated with an upward nod of the head often accompanied with a slight baring of the teeth, or clicking of the tongue, and "Yes" is indicated by a slow downward movement of the head to one side, although the younger generation increasingly use a nod for yes and a shake of the head for no.

When you compliment someone, expect to see them give a little puff breath through their lips. This is to ward off the "evil eye" of envy (Greeks are very superstitious).

Placing your hand on your heart means "Thank you."

Never raise an open palm towards someone else. While the gesture means "Stop" in many cultures, in Greece it is known as the moutza and is the equivalent of giving someone the finger.

When someone paws the air with their fingers and appears to be telling you to move back a few paces, they are actually beckoning you closer.

Touching or patting the lower lip with the index finger means "I want to tell you something" (easily mistaken for "Shhh!").

Sense of humor

A Greek scholar once said that the ancient Greek sense of humor could be summed up in a banana (meaning that it was unsophisticated). The modern sense of humor enjoys long, involved stories containing philosophical or moral elements, which can be quite impenetrable to foreigners. Humor is sharp and embedded in the culture and richness of the language and doesn't easily translate, although the warmth and vibrancy of delivery is unmistakable.

Hong Kong

National character

In Chinese, Hong Kong means "The Fragrant Harbor," and it has also been called "The Gateway to the East." In common with many Far East Asian cultures, people in Hong Kong are efficient, hardworking, and have an attitude of overcoming obstacles with time and perseverance. It is one of the most individualistic of these cultures, with a lower aversion to taking risks. However, Hong Kong remains a relationship-driven culture, where family, "face" (personal standing among one's peers), and etiquette are of vital importance. Humility and modesty are also considered desirable traits. Punctuality is very important, especially in business. An exception to this rule is when you have dinner invitations to someone's house—you should show up thirty minutes late to allow the hosts to prepare. The Chinese are very superstitious: before important decisions are made they will consider whether it is an auspicious time or day.

A brief history

Hong Kong has been an important trading region for hundreds of years. The earliest recorded Western visitor was the Portuguese explorer Jorge Álvares in 1513. European Trade with China and Hong Kong flourished, until Hong Kong was ceded to Britain under the Treaty of Nanking in 1842 after the First Opium War. It was occupied for three and a half years by the Japanese during World War II, and many inhabitants were executed. After the war there was a huge influx of Chinese refugees, escaping the newly-formed Communist government in China. Many of these people were wealthy professionals who formed the foundation for Hong Kong's growth into one of the world's most important financial and business centers. Hong Kong remained a British colony until the People's Republic of China took back its sovereignty in 1997.

Speaking

The two official languages are Chinese (the Cantonese dialect is most widely spoken) and English (the language of business and service industries).

The greeting is either a light handshake, or the Chinese bow or nod. It is customary to bow lower than those of higher status. Men and women may shake hands. Greet the senior members in a group first. Hong Kong Chinese may lower their eyes during the greeting as a sign of respect. Avoid prolonged eye contact, which will be seen as confrontational. The Chinese are very diplomatic and are reluctant to say "No." They will instead often say something like "Perhaps," or "I'll consider it." Saving face is very important in Hong

Kong, so people are ever keen to avoid situations of potential embarrassment.

Compliment others sincerely and often, show them respect, and avoid conduct that would lower their self-esteem, such as singling them out for criticism, or showing anger. Defer to those in positions of authority and the elderly.

If someone offers you a gift, it is customary to refuse it one or two times, before finally accepting it (the eastern equivalent of "You really shouldn't have!").

If someone sucks air through their teeth it means that they disagree or are unhappy with what is being said.

Body language
Keep gestures to a minimum. Chinese people use them infrequently, and may find them irritating and confusing. Avoid backslapping and other tactile gestures such as putting an arm around someone's shoulder or hugging. However, expect to see same-sex friends holding hands while walking down the street.

Maintain the same personal space as you would in Western society, but if a Chinese person comes closer, do not back away.

In a restaurant, tapping your index and middle fingers on the table twice means "Thank you." If you want more tea, turn the lid of the empty teapot upside down or hang it from the spout, and the waiter will provide a refill.

Sense of humor
Laughter and smiling is often the result of nervousness or miscomprehension. Irony and sarcasm are not easily recognized among the Chinese. If you are being sarcastic or wry, you will need to exaggerate it, since subtle attempts at irony will be misunderstood.

Hungary

National character

Hungary's national identity is shaped by the fact that it is landlocked and its inhabitants feel that their history has been one of oppression and occupation. They also have high levels of depression. The language further isolates it from its neighbors. However, with the fall of Communism the country is increasingly outward-looking and individualism is starting to flourish, although the desire for consensus is still high. Hungarians are logical, associative thinkers with a high aversion to risk. The family and personal relationships are an important focus, often with many generations living together. The majority of Hungarians are Roman Catholics and approximately 30 percent are Protestant. Hungarian hospitality is considerable, and meals are important social occasions that can last several hours. They are highly literate and numerate, as well as hardworking (many people hold down more than one job to support their family). Punctuality is very important, especially in business.

A brief history

The Hungarian people were first united under King Stephen, who reigned from 1000 to 1038 A.D., and his dynasty ruled the country for 300 years until it was conquered by the Ottoman Turks at the decisive battle of Mohács in 1526. The south of the country became part of the Ottoman Empire, while the north fell under Austrian Hapsburg rule. By the late seventeenth century the Hapsburgs expelled the Ottomans from Hungary. In 1848 the Hungarian people revolted against Hapsburg rule, but this was crushed with the help of the Russians. Hungary then became a separate state under the Hapsburg Crown ruling what became known as the Austro-Hungarian Empire, which was broken up after World War I. During World War II, Hungary sided with Nazi Germany, and became a Russian satellite during the Cold War. In 1956, the Soviets brutally suppressed a Hungarian attempt to leave the Warsaw Pact. Communism remained until 1988; the first democratic elections took place in 1990. Hungary joined NATO the following year and the EU in 2004. The country is now a multiparty republic.

Speaking

The national language is Magyar, which has different roots to other European languages, and is distantly related to Finnish. Many Hungarians also speak English and German. Hungarians are direct speakers who are often blunt when expressing their observations and beliefs. Good-natured debate is welcomed, since differences of opinion can be accommodated well without causing offense.

Acceptable topics of conversation include places and interests that have impressed you in Hungary, food and wine, soccer, chess, and horses. Avoid religion, politics, earnings, or the Versailles Treaty which so decimated the country.

Be careful when making a Hungarian toast. Mispronounce it and you could easily end up saying "To your whole rear end" ("Egész seggedre") instead of "To your health" ("Egészségedre"). Ask a Hungarian for advice on pronunciation.

Body language

Greet with a firm handshake and with good eye contact. Close friends shake hands, follow with an embrace, and then make contact first with the left cheek, and then the right. Men should wait for women to extend their hand.

Hungarians use a lot of gestures while speaking. Personal space is small and people stand close, but don't back away; they will think you are being shy (or unfriendly) and will quickly close the gap.

Hungarians can be wary of foreigners, and they take a long time to form personal relationships. Over familiarity too soon in a relationship is considered superficial and is viewed with distrust.

Make frequent eye contact that is direct and firm, indicative of honesty, attention, and sincerity.

Public displays of affection, such as kissing couples, are acceptable and commonplace.

When toasting, you should toast to the other person's success, not your own. Toasting one's own success is considered selfish and conceited.

Sense of humor

Hungarians enjoy wordplay and telling jokes (many of which have fixed characters who everyone is familiar with, such as little boy, Móricka who is obsessed with sex and being rude). They have a dry, sarcastic, even combative sense of humor and they often complain and joke about the inefficient bureaucratic system inherited from the communist era. If someone teases you jokingly, take it as a sign of friendship rather than take offense.

Iceland

National character

Iceland is referred to by many as the land of "fire and ice." It is a volcanic island with a small population of lively, welcoming, and hardy people, who are fiercely proud of their country and who enjoy a very strong sense of community and belonging—born of living in a harsh environment with little daylight. They value individuality, equality (former President Vigdís Finnbogadóttir was the first democratically-elected female head of state in the world), and tolerance, and like to play as hard as they work. Apart from partying,

favorite pastimes include outdoor activities such as hiking, fishing, skiing, camping, and bathing in geothermal springs. Icelanders are binge workers who tend to leave things to the last minute, then put in a burst of energy to meet a deadline, a throwback to times when the economy relied on fishing and everyone had to work at fever pitch to bring in the catch. They average one of the longest working days in Europe.

A recent study confirmed that Icelanders are the happiest people on earth. They are also the biggest consumers of alcohol and antidepressants—one of the many contradictions you will meet in this idiosyncratic country. In

common with the heroes of their sagas, they show an intriguing mixture of brute force and sensitivity. Icelanders place great faith in Providence, and their national motto could be: "Þetta reddast!" which means, "It'll work out in the end." They are highly educated, well-traveled, informed, and most speak good English.

A brief history

The first inhabitants of Iceland were Irish monks who arrived during the eighth century. Norsemen arrived a century later, and many other settlers came from the British Isles, many of them exiles and former slaves. During the thirteenth century the country warred for fifty years until in 1262 King Hákon Hákonarson claimed Iceland for Norway. Later still it became a Danish colony. The population was decimated by smallpox during the early eighteenth century, and there was mass emigration to the U.S. and Canada during the late nineteenth century. In 1944 it became a fully independent nation. Today it is a constitutional parliamentary democracy, and one of the least densely populated countries in the world with a population of just 300,000, of which 60 percent live in the capital, Reykjavik.

Speaking

Icelanders are direct speakers who quickly get to the point and waste little time with pleasantries and small talk. They will laugh if they find something funny, but do not generally smile politely to break the ice or to lubricate social interactions such as greetings. They are quite reserved so they are unlikely to initiate conversation with strangers, but they are friendly and welcoming if approached.

Directness and honesty are important, so don't make promises or extend invitations unless you intend to follow them through. If you say you'll look someone up the next time you're in town, they may be offended if you don't.

Icelanders will only give personal information to close friends, so don't ask personal questions unless you know someone well. Otherwise, few topics are taboo; in fact, Icelanders will often adopt a contrary view in a discussion just to stimulate debate and keep the conversation interesting. Asking advice about the nightlife in Reykjavik, or which outdoor pursuits you should try, will get people talking.

Body language

The standard greeting is a firm handshake with good eye contact. Good friends will embrace.

Icelandic people normally use closed and smaller gestures than other Europeans.

Men don't open doors for women, on the basis that the culture is very egalitarian, and women are perfectly capable of doing it themselves.

Sense of humor

As befits a well-educated, lively community, Icelandic humor can be dry, sharp, and raucous. They never take themselves too seriously, but they will tell a joke with deadpan delivery, and rarely laugh out loud. If you want to fit in, keep a cool smile on your face and save your belly laughs for when you get home. A popular Icelandic joke is that they discovered America before anyone else but decided to pass. Another example of the country's zaniness is The Icelandic Phallological Museum in Húsavík which contains a collection of over one hundred mammalian penises and penile parts.

India

National character

Religion and the caste system play a defining role in the lives of most Indians, and the social framework revolves around the extended family. Most Indians are Hindu, a poly-theistic religion that teaches the idea of karma and reincarnation. Many Hindus venerate cows and will not eat beef or wear leather. Many Hindus are vegetarian. A minority of Indians are Muslims, who will not eat pork or drink alcohol. Sikhs (about 2 percent of the population) believe in reincarnation but do not observe the caste system. Other minority religions include Christianity, Buddhism, Jainism, and Zoroastrianism.

The caste system has been used for many years and is very complicated. There are four basic levels of the system: Brahman, Kshatriya, Vaishya, and Shudra. People outside of these levels are known as Harijans (the untouchables). There are hundreds of "castes" and sub-castes within these levels into which people are born—determining their rights, the type of work they can do, who they can marry, what they can eat, and a host of other duties and regulations—which affect every aspect of their lives. Legally the government has outlawed the practice of a caste system and has a policy of affirmative action for the lower classes, but it still defines the lives of many Indians.

A brief history

India has had a continuous civilization since 2,500 B.C. Aryan tribes migrated there from the north and settled in the middle Ganges River valley. Ancient and medieval India was split into many different kingdoms which were united for the first time in the fifth century by the Gupta Dynasty. This was a golden age of Hindu culture. In the tenth and eleventh centuries India was invaded by Muslim Turks and Afghans, and in the early sixteenth century the descendants of Genghis Khan established the Mogul Dynasty, which lasted for two centuries. During the seventeenth century the British East India Company opened up trading routes to India, and by the middle of the nineteenth century Britain controlled most of present-day India, Pakistan, and Bangladesh.

In 1920 Mohandas Gandhi led a mass movement to pursue independence through a combination of non-cooperation and nonviolent resistance, which was granted on August 15, 1947. India was partitioned into largely Hindu India and Muslim Pakistan, and tension has continued between the two countries ever since.

After independence India was ruled by Mahatma Gandhi and Jawaharlal Nehru. In 1966 Nehru's daughter, Indira Gandhi, became Prime Minister. She was assassinated in 1984 by her own Sikh bodyguards in reprisal for the army's invasion of the Golden Temple in Amritsar, the chief shrine of the Sikhs. Her son, Rajiv Gandhi, succeeded her but his government was brought down under allegations of corruption (he was among those accused of receiving kickbacks from an arms manufacturer in return for a lucrative government contract). Since then, Indian politics have been characterized by fragile coalitions, assassinations, and political corruption scandals. India is a multiparty federal republic, with a prime minister as head of government, and a president as head of state.

Speaking

The national language is Hindi but English is widely spoken. There are fourteen other official languages including Bengali, Kashmiri, Punjabi, Tamil, and Urdu.

Indians are outgoing and friendly and strangers will start a conversation and ask lots of personal questions about you and your family. It acceptable for you to ask similar questions, as it displays a genuine mutual interest.

In conversation, appealing to emotions and beliefs will yield better results than express-

ing yourself using pure logic. Good topics of conversation include family-oriented themes, cricket, and movies. Don't insult Indians by comparing them with Pakistanis, and avoid bringing up the tensions between the two countries in conversation. Don't discuss religion, politics, Pakistan and the tensions in Kashmir, the caste system, poverty, or pollution: India has myriad problems and doesn't need foreigners pointing them out.

Indians are very polite and find it hard to say "No" since they are so willing to please and to avoid causing offense. Do not mistake this trait for being evasive or disingenuous. Try to avoid saying "No" and use phrases like "I'll try" or "I'll think about it," which will be interpreted as a gentle negative.

When someone offers you something (a gift, food, or drink), it is polite to refuse it once before accepting it. Never refuse an offer of hospitality, as it will be considered rude. After eating, return an offer of hospitality, rather than saying "Thank you," since there is an assumption that the hospitality was freely offered, and thanks are considered to be a form of payment.

Body language

The customary greeting is called a namaste: bow slightly at the waist while holding your palms together below your chin. Handshakes are also used in business, but the namaste is useful when you aren't sure whether physical contact is appropriate.

Avoid standing with your hands on your hips. This is an aggressive posture.

Never touch someone's head. Don't even pat a child. The head is considered the seat of the soul, and touching someone else's head, even unintentionally, is an insult.

Always wash your hands before and after a meal, and eat food with your right hand (the left hand is reserved for unclean uses such as using the bathroom). In a Hindu household, also rinse out your mouth before eating. Don't offer someone else a forkful of food from your plate, even a lover, as this will be viewed with disgust. Do not touch a communal dish with your hands or eating utensils. Be aware of any behavior that could spread germs (a breach of etiquette known as jootha): for example, to drink from a shared bottle, tip the liquid into your mouth without letting the bottle touch your lips.

Although urban centers such as Bombay or Delhi are becoming more liberal, generally you should avoid public displays of affection with members of the opposite sex, including hugging. Don't touch someone during conversation unless you know them and their preferences very well. Many Hindus and Sikhs avoid all physical contact between the sexes, and a Muslim man must ritually cleanse himself before prayer if he has touched a woman. Public affection among same sex adult friends and relations is commonplace.

Public displays of emotion are common: expect to witness arguments and emotional disagreements in public places.

Whistling, pointing or beckoning with a finger, and displaying the soles of the feet are considered rude. If your feet come into contact with someone else you should apologize, because feet are considered unclean.

Pulling your ears denotes sincerity or repentance; never touch someone else's ears.

Sense of humor

It is impossible to generalize about humor in a country as large and diverse as India, ranging from Punjabi humor that is earthy and delightfully lavatorial to the wittier word-play found in the cities and among the well educated. Humorous literary works are considered frivolous and aimed at children rather than adults.

Israel

National character

Israeli national character has been defined by Israel's need to survive as a state, due to Jews being a displaced people without a homeland for nearly two thousand years. They have suffered anti-Semitism throughout history, culminating in the holocaust during World War II when more than six million Jews lost their lives. However, Israel has no official religion and holds many Palestinians, secular Jews, and a host of other communities and sects. The largest is the Druze, a closed community of Arabs with an old syncretic faith which incorporates elements of Islam, Christianity, and Judaism. Jews are direct and warm people, who value individualism, while a strong nuclear family is the basis for social identity.

A brief history

Israel and the West Bank were the home of the Jews in biblical times. In 66 A.D. the Jews revolted against the Roman Empire, but their success was short-lived. The Romans captured Jerusalem four years later and the Jews became stateless for nearly two millennia. In the late nineteenth century Theodor Herzl established the Zionist movement in the belief that the Jews would only be safe from persecution when they had their own homeland. Many Jews started to move into Arab territory, and after World War II the modern state of Israel was created by the allies in 1948, precipitating war with the Arab countries which had lost their land as a result. In the Six-Day War of 1967 Egypt, Syria, and Jordan attacked Israel, but Israel beat them back and occupied the Egyptian Sinai, the Golan Heights, and part of Jordan. Egypt and Syria launched another attack in 1973, which also failed. In 1979 Egypt's leader Anwar al-Sadat and Israel's Menachem Begin signed a historic peace treaty. During the 1990s Israel also signed peace accords with the Palestinians, but these broke down, with both sides blaming the other for breaking the terms of the treaty. Israel pulled out of the Gaza Strip in 2005, and it is presently under the jurisdiction of the Palestinian Authority. Israel is a parliamentary multiparty democracy with a president as chief of state and a prime minister as head of government.

Speaking
The official languages are Arabic and Hebrew, although English, French, Yiddish, and Russian are also spoken.

Greet by saying "Shalom" (Peace), accompanied by a firm handshake.

Israelis are blunt speakers and even have a name for it: doogri. It is easy to mistake this directness for rudeness and belligerence, but it is also accompanied by great warmth. Interaction is intuitive, governed by relationships and feelings rather than excessive formality or displays of diplomacy. Israelis are accustomed to expressing themselves directly, without many of the social pleasantries that dilute feelings and obscure intentions in other cultures.

Israelis have strong opinions and are not afraid to air them; nevertheless you should avoid discussions of politics and religion unless you are very well informed. If you are in a heated argument and the other person breaks off, it is his way of showing that a compromise is better than conflict. Avoid discussing religion and U.S. aid to Israel.

Body language
Personal space is small. Israelis stand close, and there may be a lot of physical touching during a conversation, but don't back away; they will think you are being reserved (or unfriendly) and will quickly close the gap. Even at this close distance, you should maintain good eye contact.

Don't bring up the subject of an Orthodox Jew's wife and daughters. If he does not introduce his wife, take your lead from him. Always wait for the other party to initiate physical contact, such as a handshake.

Women should avoid physical contact, especially with Orthodox Jewish men and should never pass anything directly (including business cards), but place it on a surface such as a table for the man to pick up.

Israelis constantly gesture while speaking, but it is rude to point at another person, or use the thumbs-up gesture.

Sense of humor

There is a long tradition of verbal, witty, self-deprecating, self-referential, and anecdotal Jewish humor. A good recent example was demonstrated in February, 2006, when in response to the Jyllands-Posten Muhammad cartoons controversy, an Israeli group invited Jewish cartoonists to take part in an Israeli Anti-Semitic Cartoons Contest.

Italy

National character

Italians are warm, welcoming people who express themselves in a direct and passionate way. They express their emotions freely and often emphasize their conversation with hand gestures, even on the phone. They are tactile: hugging, kissing, and other displays of affection are spontaneous and commonplace. They are quick to welcome strangers. The central core of an Italian's life is the family, often with several generations living under one roof, and with the "Mama" (mother) as the emotional hub. Sons often live at home well into their twenties, and the extended family plays a big part in the life of a growing child.

Mealtimes are important occasions for social interaction—good food and good company are to be savored and never rushed. A typical Italian meal may involve up to four courses: an antipasto ("before the meal": often platters of cheeses and sliced meats), primo ("first course": a pasta or rice dish), secondo ("second course": usually consisting of meat or fish), and dessert. Italian food is always very simply prepared, with an emphasis on using fresh ingredients of the best quality.

Italian bureaucracy is akin to that of the

French. The Italians have over two millennia of laws, and when new laws are added, old ones are rarely removed. Italians are proud of their artistic heritage as a country that has produced some of the world's greatest artists.

A brief history

Early Latin/Italic tribes were present in Italy as early as 3,000 years ago. Etruscan culture developed in Italy after about 800 B.C. and this was followed by the Greeks. The Roman republic was founded in 509 B.C., and its empire stretched from Europe to Africa. The Roman Empire had a profound influence

in shaping European social, legal, political, artistic, and military culture. After the fall of the Roman Empire, Italy suffered repeated invasions from other countries and became divided into a large number of independent cities, provinces, and islands.

The Renaissance, a period of great cultural change and achievement in Europe that marked the transition between Medieval and Early Modern Europe, began in Italy. Italian Renaissance cultural achievements included works by great writers such as Petrarch and Machiavelli, artists such as Michelangelo and Leonardo da Vinci, and great works of architecture, such as St. Peter's Basilica in Rome

Italy finally emerged as a nation state in 1871 with a unified monarchy, which ruled until 1946. During World War II the fascist dictator Benito Mussolini controlled Italy's government and supported Hitler. Today Italy is governed as a parliamentary representative democratic republic, with the Prime Minister as the head of government.

Speaking

Attempt to speak the language and your effort will be appreciated; you are more likely to elicit gentle laughter than to cause any offense. In a gathering of Italians it is common for everyone to speak at once, and interrupting one another is a sign of lively debate rather than rudeness.

Asking someone you have just met about their profession is considered clumsy and even rude. "What do you do?" is a very poor choice of conversational ice breaker. Safe topics of conversation for a first meeting are highlighting what has impressed you during your stay, or enquiring where the other person is from.

Italians greet each other by saying "Buon giorno" (Good day) during the morning and "Buona sera" (Good evening) during the late afternoon and evening. However, when answering the phone they say "Pronto," which means "Ready."

Body language

The Italians use the expression bella figura which means literally "the beautiful figure," and refers to the importance in Italian culture of presenting a good image, including appearance, conduct, and good manners. Italians are extremely quick in recognizing even the subtlest hints and gestures.

Pointing downwards with your index finger, with the thumb at right angles then waggling it up and down, means "Yes or no?"

Sticking an index finger in the air means "Attention! I want to speak." This isn't a rude gesture, since interrupting and interjecting are all part of the lively and distinctly non-linear conversation.

To show that you dislike something, place your hand on your stomach and make a disapproving face.

To express anger or frustration, rub your chin with your fingers and then flick them forward.

Holding the palm flat and facing up, then moving it out from the chest and back from the elbow means "That's annoying."

The OK sign made with thumb and index finger with both hands means "Perfect!"

Sense of humor

Italian humor is often strident, flirtatious, visual, and peppered with double entendre (a recent mainstream Italian TV commercial featured a male porn star celebrating the great taste of potato chips. In Italian "pata-tina" (potato chip) is also a common nickname for a woman's private parts.

However, as the distinguished Italian director Mario Monicelli describes Italian humor in movies: "The themes that make one laugh always stem from poverty, hunger, misery, old age, sickness, and death. These are the themes that make Italians laugh anyway . . . The more dramatic and tragic the moment, the more material there will be for irony and comedy."

Japan

National character

Japanese people have a strong work ethic and desire for consensus. There is a great pressure to conform and to maintain a good public image. Loss of "face" is a big deal. Anything that causes a person to lose face diminishes their reputation as well as that of the group to which they belong, such as family or company. This in turn lowers their self-esteem, since individuals judge themselves by how they are viewed by everybody else. Culture is dominated by etiquette, but so long as you show consideration for others and the group identity and deference to your superiors and elders, you will not go far wrong. Punctuality, politeness, and composure are essential at all times.

A brief history

Situated in the Pacific Ocean, off the coast of eastern Asia, Japan is made up of four main mountainous islands and lots of smaller ones. Its first inhabitants date back more than 100,000 years. The first distinct culture were the Jomon people, who were hunter-gatherers, followed by the Yayoi, who are more closely identified with the modern Japanese.

Japan came under the rule of a single emperor in the seventh century. Much of Japanese history has been characterized by internal warring between clans, while the country remained cut off from the rest of the world until the nineteenth century.

After its defeat in World War II, Japan rebuilt its economy which boomed during the 1970s and 1980s, although it has stagnated since. It has a parliamentary democracy under a constitutional monarch, with an emperor as chief of state.

Speaking

The Japanese dislike public displays of emotion, and first meetings may be quite serious. Never show your anger or raise your voice, as this will cause much offense and loss of face. Your anger will be met with either a poker face or a nervous smile or giggle, but be certain that your indiscretion will mark you down as questionable.

Any behavior which singles out individuals, such as being critical or paying compliments, is likely to cause embarrassment. Paying compliments to a group is also unacceptable since it would give the impression that the individual paying the compliment believes they are sufficiently important to be able to pass judgment on an entire group.

The Japanese desire to please means that they find it very difficult to say "No," preferring instead a gentle negative such as "I'll consider it" or "This could be very difficult." Be sensitive to this subtlety of communication; often what is left unsaid is as important as what is said. Silence speaks loudly between the words. If someone cannot answer your question, they are likely to respond with respectful silence rather than admit that they don't know.

When someone closes their eyes or crosses their arms while you are speaking it is a sign that they are considering what you are saying. This does not express disinterest.

It is important to nod while someone is speaking to indicate that you are listening and understand what they are saying.

Body language

Japanese people often shake hands with their western counterparts, but the traditional greeting is the bow from the waist, with eyes lowered and palms held flat against the thighs, as an expression of respect and humility between men, women, and children. The person of lower status bows slightly lower than the person of higher status. If you are unsure assume they are of higher status. A bow is often used for apologies, which can sometimes feel like a national pastime. Japanese people are so used to bowing that they even do it while speaking on the phone.

The Japanese use subtle facial expressions, in keeping with the emphasis of gathering one's thoughts before speaking, rather than expressing gut reactions. Overt displays of emotion suggest insincerity or weakness. The Japanese believe that the actions one takes over the long run are ultimately of greater value than words.

Eye contact is used to express deference. Not looking into the eyes of a superior, or even facing in a different direction, is common.

Receiving and giving gifts is done with two hands, held out in front, with a bow.

Smiling doesn't always express amusement; Japanese people often giggle to disguise nervousness or embarrassment; head scratching is often used in the same way.

Waving the hand, thumb towards the face, back and forth as if fanning in short strokes, means "No, not me," or "No, thank you," depending on the situation.

Where Westerners point to their chests as if to ask, "Me?" the Japanese point to the tips of their noses.

Sniffing and spitting in public are acceptable, but paradoxically blowing your nose is not (and carrying a sodden tissue or handkerchief in your pocket is considered unsanitary). No one knows why this is so, but equally intriguing is why sniffing in the West is considered more distasteful than loudly expelling the contents of your nose into a tissue.

Sense of humor

The Japanese sense of humor can at first seem impenetrable, since it is so deeply imbedded in the language and culture. A large proportion of Japanese humor is verbal (Japanese has vast numbers of words that sound exactly the same), but slapstick and the grotesque are also popular, as in the ubiquitous prank TV shows that place unsuspecting victims in compromising situations. Straight-faced, dry humor will not work here at all.

Mexico

National character

Ninety percent of Mexico is Roman Catholic and every town and village has its own patron saint. The family is the most important social structure in the country, so nepotism is widespread and accepted as the norm. Having a well-connected network of family, friends, and memberships is the best way to get on in Mexican society. Mexicans are very risk averse, and will view outsiders in terms of their contribution to the group rather than their individual expertise. There is a huge division between rich and poor, but Mexico has a large middle class. Society is male-dominated and masculinity and dignity are important components of a man's credibility and status. The pace of life is slow, and it is important to spend time building relation-ships if you want to do business here.

A brief history

There is evidence of human habitation in Mexican since 20,000 years B.C. There have been many native cultures, of which five stand out: the Olmecs, Teotihuacans, Toltecs, Mayans, and finally the Aztec culture, which was conquered by the Spanish conquistador Hernán Cortés in the early sixteenth century. Mexico was called "New Spain" during its colonial period until it achieved indepen-dence in 1821. This was preceded by the War of Independence (1810 to 1821), which was initiated by the priest Miguel Hidalgo on September 16, 1810, Mexico's National Day. In 1824 Mexico adopted a constitution, making it a federal republic under its first president Guadalupe Victoria. In 1836, Texas broke away from Mexico, causing a war be-tween Mexico and the United States, in which Mexico was defeated and forfeited present day California, Arizona, New Mexico, and Texas to the U.S. From 1876 the dictatorial rule of Porfirio Diaz sowed the seeds of the Mexican Revolution of 1911, led by Emiliano Zapata and Francisco Villa, and a new Consti-tution was approved in 1917. Mexico fought against Germany in World War II, and was of the founding members of United Nations in 1945. The United State of Mexico is a federal republic, with a president as head of the government.

Speaking

Spanish is the main language and English is the most spoken second language. About one-third of the population speaks (some-times exclusively) the indigenous Indian languages of the Aztecs and Maya. Try to speak a little Spanish and it will be much appreciated.

While Mexicans are direct speakers and very open about expressing their emotions, their desire to please means that they find it

very difficult to say "No," preferring instead to use the cover-all "mañana" which means, "Tomorrow." This can seem like stalling or laziness, but try to see it from its more positive perspective.

Mexicans may try to attract your attention by saying "Psst-psst," which is not considered rude.

The best way to get to know someone is to show great interest in their family and children. Be an active listener and allow others to tell you all about themselves, which they will do readily. Other good topics of conversation include Mexican sights, soccer, baseball, and bullfighting. Do not talk about illegal Mexican immigrants to other countries.

Mexicans have a tendency to repeat questions such as "How are you?" to show that they are genuinely interested in you.

Use a medium to loud voice, which shows that you are an engaged and interested conversationalist; a quiet voice may be misinterpreted as disinterest or boredom.

Body language

A Mexican handshake is a brisk, firm snap. Say "Buenos dias/tardes/noches" for "Good morning/afternoon/evening or night" or "Hola" for a more informal "Hi." Women often greet by patting each other on the right forearm, rather

than shaking hands. At a party acknowledge everyone in the room with a brief nod and shake hands with each person as you are introduced to them.

Friends greet each other with a bear hug (abrazo) with much back slapping. Mexicans make friends quickly, so you may find yourself on the receiving end of an abrazo after only a few meetings.

Winking and whistling (called the piripo) is common between men and women on meeting, as well as cheek-kissing.

Personal space is small. Mexicans stand close, and there may be a lot of physical touching during a conversation, but don't back away; they will think you are being reserved (or unfriendly) and will quickly close the gap.

Keep eye contact short and infrequent, especially with elders. Prolonged eye contact is considered confrontational. Women's eye contact is less frequent than men's.

Sense of humor

Mexican love telling jokes and stories, often at their own expense, but they do not understand sarcasm and irony, and will take it literally and become easily offended by your perceived negativity.

Morocco

National character

Morocco is a modern, progressive and semi-democratic Muslim country. Personal and familial honor and dignity are very important considerations, and Moroccans are conscious of how their behavior and that of others impacts them. When someone behaves inappropriately and brings shame on themselves and their family, it is known as Hshuma. The family is the most important social unit, the individual is always subordinate to the family or group, and nepotism is viewed positively.

A brief history

The earliest inhabitants arrived 15,000 years ago during the Paleolithic era. Around 1,100 B.C. the Phoenicians established trading posts, and during the first century A.D. the Berber kingdom became established in the northwest. It became part of the Roman Empire until their withdrawal in 253. The area was occupied by the Vandals, then the Byzantines. Islam was introduced in the seventh century A.D. During the eleventh century the Berber dynasty of Almoravids extended their territory as far as Libya, Spain, and deep into the Sahara. During the Middle Ages the country stagnated culturally and economically, until the golden age of Morroco began at the end of the sixteenth century. This lasted until relations with Europe were cut off during the early

nineteenth century, sending the region into decline, as it ceded territory to Spain. French Colonialism began in 1904 and ended in March 1956 with Moroccan independence. Morocco signed the Euro-Mediterranean Partnership with the European Union in 1996, and has made progress towards democratization, but there is still state suppression of dissidents, as well as control over media and other organizations.

Speaking

The official language is Arabic, about a third of the population speaks Berber, and French is widely spoken and is often the language of business. Many Moroccans in the north of the country speak Spanish, and English is growing in popularity.

Moroccans are initially wary of strangers, but once you have gained someone's trust, their friends will treat you with the same confidence.

Do not look women in the eye and do not talk to members of the opposite sex who are strangers; it will be interpreted as a sexual advance.

Maintain good eye contact while speaking with men, as a sign of trustworthiness and attentiveness. If a woman speaks to you without much eye contact, take her lead and reciprocate out of politeness. Morocco is a very hierarchical country, so some men will minimize eye contact as a sign of deference.

It is acceptable to inquire about someone's family in order to break the ice; avoid subjects such as politics, religion, and women's rights, and never criticize the King or pass negative judgment on the country.

During a conversation, you may find that other people agree with you even though they are not fully convinced of your argument; it is often necessary to revisit the topic later to find out their true feelings.

During conversation a speaker will often be interrupted while everyone else offers their opinion; take it as a sign of lively debate rather than rudeness and inattentiveness.

Body language

Greet by shaking hands (with moderate pressure) and saying "Salam," or "Peace be unto you." This is often followed by tapping the hand on the heart, and an extended exchange of inquiries after health, family, friends, and other matters. Close friends of the same sex often kiss each other one on one cheek and twice on the other. Wait for a woman to extend her hand before shaking it, otherwise bow your head slightly in greeting.

Personal space is very close; don't back away even if you feel that your personal space is being invaded, as this will be interpreted as rejection. Hand and facial gestures are the norm.

When eating, pass plates of food with your right hand; the left hand is reserved for unclean uses such as going to the bathroom.

Male friends often hold hands while walking together, as do female friends. However, public displays of affection between the opposite sexes are unacceptable.

Sense of humor

Avoid jokes about religion, sex, and politics. While jokes on these subjects undoubtedly exist in Morocco, a female journalist recently published an article discussing Moroccan humor and included some examples which mocked the king, Islamist imams, and attitudes toward women. She has since been charged with bringing "insult to the Islamic faith" and "publication and distribution of writings that are contrary to the morals and mores" of the country.

Avoid these subjects, as well as sarcasm or critical humor unless you know someone very well and are sure that they won't object. If in doubt, stick to clean jokes that you know will not cause offense.

The Netherlands

National character

Dutch society is egalitarian, individualistic, pragmatic, and modern. The people are modest, tolerant, and hard working. Compromise and consensus are very important. Everyone has the right to make their own choices, so long as they do not draw undue attention to themselves, interfere with or show intolerance towards the rights and interests of others. Ostentatious behaviors—such as boasting or visible displays of wealth—are unwelcome.

The Dutch are attracted to direct logic and facts over subjective emotions. Punctuality is very important, especially in business, and you should arrive on time to social events.

A brief history

The Romans occupied the country south of the river Rhine and fought Germanic tribes and Celts there. After the fall of the Roman Empire the Netherlands became part of Charlemagne's Frankish kingdom. Thereafter the country was governed by a succession of European rulers, while its trade and industry flourished. It fell into Spanish control in the sixteenth century until Calvanist Dutch rebels led a revolt against Philip II of Spain. After a war that had lasted eighty years, independence was declared July, 26, 1581.

By the seventeenth century the country was the foremost trading nation in the world, before being overtaken by Britain, France, and Germany.

The French occupied the Netherlands from the beginning of the nineteenth century until 1848 when its monarchy was replaced by a parliamentary democracy with a constitutional monarch. The country was occupied by the Nazis during World War II. Today the Netherlands is a modern, industrialized nation.

Speaking

The Dutch speak directly. Try to be direct and precise with your speech and avoid hyperbole and superlatives, which will be viewed with confusion and suspicion. If in doubt, favor understatement: for example, saying something is "Not bad" or "OK" can be considered as praise.

Raising your voice or using excessive gesturing is unwelcome. For example, if you saw someone at a distance and wanted to attract their attention or to say hello, shouting a greeting would attract plenty of disapproving looks.

Compliments are unwelcome since they highlight the individual above the group, and are considered as hollow flattery rather than genuine praise.

When getting to know people, do not be over-friendly too soon. Be restrained and dignified at first, and don't crack too many jokes. Friendship and trust are built slowly. Avoid asking personal questions as privacy is very important. Safe topics of conversation include where you are from, local Dutch issues, and asking advice about interesting sites you should visit. Avoid stereotypes such as drugs, clogs, and windmills.

The Dutch can be blunt and critical without meaning to offend. Directness is much appreciated; if you hold back your opinions because you are afraid of causing offense, you may be viewed as being averse to plain speaking. The Dutch are ready to share their opinions and seldom take offense if you share yours.

Do not refer to the country as Holland, which is only a small part of the Netherlands.

Body language

Body language is reserved and understated, but not casual. For example, talking with your hands in your pockets is impolite. Moderate hand gestures are an acceptable sign of openness. Personal space is wide.

Expect a lot of eye contact. If you look away while talking or stare at the ground people may think you are disinterested or lying.

Tapping the side of your head with your index finger indicates that someone is crazy, and is a very rude gesture. By contrast, tapping just above the ear indicates that someone is intelligent.

Nodding the head is accepted as a sign of agreement, while shaking the head suggests disapproval rather than disagreement.

Sense of humor

Dutch humor is subtle and relies on irony and sarcasm and witty remarks rather than slapstick. It can often be quite black and bordering on insult at the expense of self and others. Dutch television advertising plays to this sense of humor, and is often self-mocking and ironic.

Humor is often political and based on sophisticated word-play (for example using alliteration for emphasis or compounding words together to make new words for comic effect). Even a comic like Hans Teeuwen who is sexually explicit and challenges political correctness displays this characteristically Dutch fascination with linguistic acrobatics. When making fun of other nations, the Dutch often target the supposed stupidity of the Belgians, and the perceived arrogance of the Germans (orange Nazi helmets were on sale for Dutch soccer fans during the last World Cup).

New Zealand

National character

New Zealand has a population of about four million people, most of who live in major cities. The society is fiercely egalitarian, so wealth and social status are less important than being approachable and trustworthy. While individual achievement is encouraged, "tall poppy" syndrome (also known as the great Kiwi clobbering machine) is a feature of New Zealand culture. This means that those who try to pull rank or boast about their abilities are quickly brought down to size, usually with humor. Kiwis are laid-back but direct communicators, who respect honesty and down-to-earth interaction. Many are well traveled and forward thinking and are not risk averse. Initially reserved, they are naturally accepting and trusting unless given good evidence to the contrary. They are very concerned about protecting the environment, so border controls are very stringent, and there are large fines for importing food, animals, or other natural products.

A brief history

The earliest inhabitants of New Zealand were the Maori, who arrived from Polynesia around 900 A.D. The first European settlers were the Dutch, in 1642, followed by British explorer Captain James Cook in 1769. The major difference between Australian and Kiwi history is that New Zealand was not a penal colony, and most of the incomers arrived voluntarily. However, increased British colonization led to Britain annexing the country in 1838, granting self-government in 1852. New Zealand fought on the side of the Allies during the two World Wars. Today it is a constitutional monarchy, with a governor-general representing the British monarch.

Speaking

The two official languages are English and Maori. Although New Zealanders are a bit more formal than Australians, you will frequently hear the informal greeting "G'Day." You can also use this, but don't overdo it, or you may appear patronizing. A more formal greeting is "How do you do?" The Maori word for hello is "Tena koe" when addressing one person and "Tena koutou kotoa" when addressing more than one person.

Don't confuse New Zealanders with Australians. They are as different as Canadians and Americans. Good topics of conversation include sport, especially rugby and sailing, at which New Zealand excels. Don't ask personal questions about salary, or bring up political issues such as the Treaty of Waitangi (1840), which many Maori feel has been repeatedly breached; nuclear power; and the introduction of genetically modified foods.

Body language

Greet with a firm handshake while maintaining good eye contact. Many indigenous New Zealanders (Maori) treat prolonged eye contact as confrontational, whereas non-indigenous New Zealanders use eye contact that is direct and firm, indicative of honesty, attention, and sincerity. The traditional Maori greeting, called a hongi, is usually only used at formal Maori events and not in everyday life. This greeting involves pressing noses together with eyes closed while making a "Mm-mm" sound.

Personal body space is quite wide, so allow at least two feet of space.

Kiwi men are not very tactile with each other, so don't put your arm around another man or engage in any other physical "buddy" behavior unless you know him very well.

Cover your mouth when you yawn or sneeze. Never chew gum in public.

Ask permission before attempting to photograph someone.

Sense of humor

Humor is often used to demean those who are too serious or those who have an inflated opinion of themselves, and is often self-depreciating. To make a joke at a friend's expense is a sign of a healthy friendship. If you are teased, you are expected to stand up for yourself and reply in kind, with good humor, rather than take offense.

There is a friendly though sarcastic rivalry between the North Islanders (mostly targeted at Aucklanders) and South Islanders, and some jokes reflect this.

Norway

National character

Norwegians are proud and egalitarian people who consider themselves less formal than their Scandinavian neighbors (they particularly think the Swedes are very conventional). They value tolerance, diversity, and gender equality. Their high standard of living is made possible by huge oil and gas reserves and a relatively small hard-working population of less than five million with a high level of education.

Like the rest of Scandinavia, Norwegians seek to minimize social difference with high taxes to provide a strong welfare state, as there is a responsibility to help those who are less fortunate. Social categories are defined by education and occupation rather than income groups. Well-off Norwegians do not flaunt their wealth. Also, displays of material superiority are discouraged. For this reason informality and humility are essential virtues.

A brief history

The earliest Norwegians were hunter-gatherers living 10,000 years ago. From about 5,000 B.C. they started to turn to agriculture. Norway had trading links with the Roman Empire. But their most famous period of its history was the age of the Vikings (c. 800 to 1050 A.D.), who conducted raids throughout Europe, marking the end of the prehistoric period in Norway. During the reign of King Håkon V, in the 1200s, Oslo became Norway's capital. During the Middle Ages most of Scandinavia fell under the control of Denmark, but in 1815, after the Napoleonic Wars, Norway was taken away from Denmark and given to Sweden. The country suffered a huge economic depression as many of the wealthier middle class citizens in the country's southeast region went bankrupt. The Norwegian nobility was subsequently abolished, and economic recovery occurred from 1830 with the growth of industrialization.

In August of 1905 an independence referendum took place in which Norwegians voted overwhelmingly to end the Union with Sweden. This was granted peacefully, and the Danish prince Håkon became the first king of the newly independent country.

Norway was occupied by Nazi Germany during World War II, despite its neutrality. After the war it joined NATO in 1949 and the European Union in 1994. It is a multiparty constitutional monarchy with a prime minister as head of government.

Speaking

The official language is Norwegian, and there are two types of written language: "Bok-

mal" (Book Norwegian) and Nynorsk (New Norwegian).

Greet everyone in the room, men and women, with a firm handshake with good eye contact and say "God dag" (Good day).

Norwegians are direct and straightforward communicators who appreciate directness in conversation. Although they can appear reserved at first, they will quickly warm to you once trust has been established. Interrupting someone while they are speaking is considered rude.

Don't lump Norwegians in with the other Scandinavian cultures; be sensitive to the country's uniqueness. Safe topics of conversation include the weather, sports, and international politics (Norwegians are very internationalist), as well as family, work and place of origin. They are hardworking people, therefore they would resent any implication that their standard of living is solely due to the lucky accident of discovering North Sea oil during the 1960s.

Body language
Avoid backslapping and other tactile gestures such as putting an arm around someone's shoulder or hugging. Allow plenty of personal space between yourself and others.

Although raising the middle finger is rude, most other hand gestures are acceptable—but don't point at others while talking. Norwegian body language is minimal.

Although Norwegians have a reputation for being able to party, they frown upon behavior that is disruptive and draws attention, so save your gregarious behavior for the beer-soaked weekends.

Sense of humor
Humor is, as expected, language specific, but sarcasm is common, as well as making fun of other Scandinavian cultures. For example this joke implies that Swedes are unable to process higher-order thinking: A Swede comes into a bookstore. The shopkeeper asks him, "Do you want something light or would you prefer heavier reading?" The Swede replies, "It doesn't matter, I have the car outside."

Pakistan

National character

Pakistani society is multilingual and predominantly Muslim. The northwestern region which borders Afghanistan is the most conservative area, and is dominated by regional tribal customs. In contrast the cities such as Karachi, Lahore, Hyderabad are more liberal, although religious observance is an integral part of life and all aspects of Pakistani beliefs and behavior are subject to Islamic law.

The extended family is the most important societal structure. Women are expected to get married and leave the family home between the ages of eighteen and twenty-five, while one or more of the sons will stay with his parents his whole life and look after them in old age.

A brief history

Pakistan, which means "land of the pure," was created as a separate Muslim state in 1947 when the British partitioned India, but its rich heritage dates back thousands of years to the Indus Valley Civilization (3000 to 2500 B.C.). From 1500 B.C. Aryan tribes migrated there from the north. Medieval Pakistan was part of the many different kingdoms that constituted India, which were united for the first time in the fifth century by the Gupta Dynasty. In the tenth and eleventh centuries Pakistan was in-

vaded by Muslim Turks and Afghans, and in the early sixteenth century the descendants of Genghis Khan established the Mogul Dynasty, which lasted for two centuries.

Pakistan fell under British colonial rule and became a separate Muslim state during the partition created from Punjab and Bengal on August 14, 1947. It became a fully independent republic in 1956. East and West Pakistan fought each other in 1970, when more than a million East Pakistanis were killed, and East Pakistan seceded as the independent state of Bangladesh after India invaded to drive back the West Pakistanis. Pakistan is a multiparty federal Islamic Republic whose government is dominated by the military. There is limited freedom of the press and concerns about human rights abuses.

Speaking

The customary greeting is a handshake with the words "Assalaam-u-Alaikum" (May peace be upon you); your reply should be "Waalaikum assalaam" (And peace also upon you). Close friends of the same sex may embrace. Women rarely greet each other with a handshake; they usually hug or kiss. Men should not shake hands with women, although it is acceptable for a foreign woman to shake hands with a man.

Inquiring about family is acceptable and

polite, but do not show too much interest in a person's female relatives. Good topics for conversation include local and regional history and sports, especially cricket. Avoid talking about the country's poverty, nuclear testing, hostility with India (and the disputed region of Kashmir), the "war on terror," the equality of women, religion, and politics.

Body language

It is customary to refuse a gift or an offer of food and drink several times before accepting it. Often the other person will place it in your hand to encourage you to accept. Don't accept food and drink from strangers on public transport, as there have been several cases of drugging and mugging.

Public display of anger is discouraged. You should always be polite and respectful.

Do not look women in the eye and do not talk to members of the opposite sex who are strangers. This will be interpreted as a sexual advance.

Eat and pass plates of food with your right hand. (The left hand is reserved for unclean uses, such as going to the bathroom.) Public displays of affection between members of the opposite sex are out of the question, including hugging to say hello. A man should not touch a woman unless she makes the

first move (offers her hand to be shaken, for example). Muslim men must ritually cleanse themselves before prayer if they touch a woman.

Touch between members of the same sex is acceptable, such as putting a hand around someone's shoulder or holding hands.

Don't gesture with individual fingers (e.g. pointing): use an open hand instead. Don't snap your fingers, whistle, wink, or show the soles of your feet or point them at someone else. Gesturing with a closed fist is considered obscene.

Women always take precedence in lines and seating.

Sense of humor

Pakistanis are able to laugh at themselves as well as others; but do not make jokes about sex or anything rude, and steer clear of politics, ethnicity, and religion. Someone once asked Pakistan cricket captain Inzamam-ul-Haq why he wins the toss so often. His reply: "I practice a lot."

Poland

National character

In the past Poland's national character has been defined by living between the bear and the wolf—sandwiched as it is between Russia and Germany—and years of Communist rule. Since the fall of Russian Communism, Poland's values are becoming increasingly "Western," although it is still quite male-dominated. Although Poland was Communist for a long time, the society is very class-based and hierarchical: status is derived from the family and people tend to socialize very much with their own kind.

The culture is a mixture of contradictions, of apparent formality and warmth, risk-avoiding and risk-taking. Ninety-nine percent of the population is Catholic, and a successful family life (Poland has one of the lowest divorce rates in Europe) and good friends are highly valued, and great respect is paid to one's elders. Strangers will be welcomed, but Poles really only let their hair down among close friends and family.

A brief history

Slavic tribes settled in what was to become Poland more than 2,000 years ago, and the country was named after one of these tribes, the Polane ("plain people"—Poland is very flat). Poland officially came into existence in the tenth century under the Catholic King Mieszko I. Throughout its history it has been under military threat from its neighbors and has been swallowed up in the German, Russian, and Austrian empires.

After World War I, Poland broke away from the Russian empire—only to fall into the hands of the Germans during World War II. Over six million Poles died during German occupation, and then Poland became a Communist state after the war. Public opposition led by Lech Walesa and the organization "Solidarity" led to the political liberalization and the transition to a market economy. Its first free elections were held in 1990. Today the country is an independent multiparty democracy, a member of NATO, and the European Union.

Speaking

Poles speak quite softly, so maintain an equivalent vocal level in conversation and avoid raising your voice in public. Don't yell across the street to attract someone's attention.

It is common to say "Smachnago" (Good eating) before a meal and "Na zdrowie" (Cheers) before drinking.

Someone will almost certainly invite you to try repeating the tongue twister: "W

Szczebrzeszynie chrzḐszcz brzmi w trzcinie" (which means "In the town of Szczebrzeszyn a beetle buzzes in the reed"), which is tricky even for Poles to recite.

Do not be afraid to express your ideas. A frank exchange of opinions is a natural part of discourse without threatening rapport.

Body language

The Poles are very sensitive to body language, so it is important to maintain good eye contact and be aware of how you are presenting yourself.

Greet people with a firm handshake with good eye contact, and say "Czesc" (Hello) or "Do widzenia" (Goodbye). Women and close friends greet each other with cheek kisses (usually three) and a lot of hugging. Occasionally Polish men kiss each other on the cheek, and men may kiss women on the hand.

Compliments are welcome. However, as with all compliments, they should be appropriate and sincere.

Hand gestures are minimal, but there is no need to restrict your own gesturing, if that is what you're used to.

Do not sit with one ankle resting on the other knee and do not speak with your hands in your pockets.

Flicking the finger against the neck means "Let's have a drink (of vodka)."

Poles have a fraternal toast called a Bruderszaft, which it would be very rude to decline. Two people raise a toast together and then interlock arms and down their drinks. Finally they exchange kisses and names: such as "Call me Jacek."

Men should open doors for women and allow them to pass through first.

Sense of humor

Polish humor is sophisticated and at the ironic, sarcastic, word-play end of the comedy spectrum. The worldwide bestselling Polish author of science fiction, philosophy and satire, Stanislaw Lem (1921 to 2006), was a master of Polish neologisms and convoluted wordplay.

Portugal

National character

Portugal has a homogeneous population of about ten million people, with two thirds living in the coastal fourth of the country, and a fifth living in the capital, Lisbon. Most people identify themselves as Roman Catholic, although only about one-third attend church on a daily basis. Nevertheless the church and the family are two defining influences in the country. Portuguese people are easygoing, welcoming, and friendly. Those in the north are more formal and conservative, while southerners are more laid-back. They are hard workers, with more than a third of the country employed in industry, and nearly half in the service industries. Although machismo is part of the culture, women account for more than half of all people in higher education.

A brief history

The western part of the Iberian Peninsula that is now Portugal was occupied by a culture called the Lusitanos, from whom the Portuguese are thought to be descended. The region

was occupied by the Romans, and later by the Moors. In 1140 Portugal became an independent nation under King Alfonso Henriques, and during subsequent centuries the country built (and then lost) a large colonial empire in Africa, Latin America, India, and the Far East, owing to the explorations of men like Prince Henry the Navigator, Vasco da Gama (who made the first sea voyage from Europe to the East), Pedro Alvares Cabral (the first European explorer to arrive in South America), and Fernão Magellan (the first European to cross the Pacific Ocean and to circumnavigate the globe).

In 1580 Portugal came under Spanish control until it seceded in 1640. It was then ruled by the Braganza dynasty until the mid-nineteenth century. Portugal supported the Allies during World War I. Between the wars, a right-wing dictatorship led by Antonio de Oliveira Salazar and influenced by the fascism of Benito Mussolini in Italy took power, but the country remained neutral during World War II. Salazar remained in power until 1968, and six years later his successor, Marcello Caetano, was deposed in a bloodless military coup. Since then the country has followed the typical Western European model of multiparty parliamentary democracy. Portugal joined the European Union in 1986.

Speaking

Portuguese people are very interested in and welcoming towards strangers, so initial conversation should flow smoothly, especially if you ask about Portuguese culture and history. They are open and direct speakers who say what they mean, and you will be expected to do the same. Avoid talking about politics and government.

The Portugese can be quite emotional and subjective in their reasoning, so when speaking try to appeal to these qualities, rather than objective logic. For example, make an analogy or word picture that illustrates your point, rather than laying down the dry facts.

Body language

On first meeting greet everyone in the group with a handshake, although don't make it too firm. Women usually kiss each other on both cheeks, and men often kiss female friends this way.

Eye contact is strong and prolonged. At first this may make you feel uncomfortable, but you should try to match the level of eye contact, or you may be viewed as unfriendly or untrustworthy.

Flicking the hand under the chin means "I don't know" or "I don't understand." If you see the same gesture being used with just the thumb it means that something no longer exists or has died.

You will be judged more on your body language (smiling and open gestures) and congeniality than on what you say or your perceived status.

Displays of affection and emotions are acceptable in public. Physical or verbal punishment of a child, even by the parents, is unacceptable.

Sense of humor

The Portuguese have a wonderful sense of humor that is direct and open; think more about belly laughs than making wry observations. It is acceptable to use humor even when you don't know someone very well, as it helps build a rapport. Don't take yourself too seriously.

Romania

National character

Romanian temperament is more akin to that of the Mediterranean than Eastern Europe, and they identify strongly with Italy and France. Between the wars Bucharest was known as the "Paris of the East." Romanians are intense, independent, spontaneous, fiercely nationalistic, and confident risk takers who are very open to outside influences and information. They welcome strangers with a self-assured curiosity and legendary hospitality. The family is the foundation of the social structure which is hierarchical; therefore much respect is shown towards the elderly.

A brief history

The territory of Romania has been inhabited since ancient times. The Getae (also known as Daci) were defeated by the Romans in the second century A.D., and Romanians trace their descent to this period. Romania as we know it today was formed from the union of Moldavia and Wallachia, after these regions were freed from the Ottoman Empire. Romania was neutral at the start of World War I, then it joined the Allies, but the country was occupied by the Central Powers. Despite protection from Russia, it surrendered in May 1918. After the collapse of the Central Powers, Romania occupied Bessarabia,

Transylvania, and part of Hungary. During World War II, Romania helped the Italians invade Yugoslavia, and fought with the Nazis against Russia, but switched sides when the Red Army invaded Romania in August 1944. A communist government was established and Gheorghe Gheorghiu-Dej took power, followed by the brutally suppressive dictator Nicolae CeauÐescu, who ruled for twenty-four years until he was overthrown by a revolution in 1989 and publicly hanged. Today Romania is a multiparty republic with a president as head of state and a prime minister as head of the government. It joined NATO in 2004, and the EU in January 2007.

Speaking

The official language is Romanian, a Latin language that has much in common with Italian, French, and Spanish. French and English are also widely used, and Hungarian is spoken by about 7 percent of the population.

Ordinary conversation can become quite loud and passionate; this is rarely a sign that an argument is taking place.

Good topics of conversation include local and national places of interest, soccer, and wine, as well as more personal interests that touch people's lives, such as family background. However, don't bring up the Roma (Gypsies), the Communist era, or Romania being one of the poorest countries in Europe—and be discreet about your own salary, since it will probably be several times greater than that of your hosts.

Personal space is close, and eye contact is less frequent than in the West. Take your lead from your hosts, and be assured that you are being listened to, even if sporadic eye contact may suggest otherwise.

Body language

Greet with a firm handshake. Male acquaintances often kiss a woman's hand, and close male friends and family cheek-kiss and hug. "Buna ziua" means "Good day." Romanians shake hands frequently, at each meeting throughout the day.

Romanians use a lot of gestures and facial expressions, although not as many as in Mediterranean countries.

Poking the thumb between the index and middle fingers of a clenched fist is an insult.

Older men will pull out chairs, offer their seats, and open doors for women. They will also kiss women's hands upon greeting (foreigners are not expected to kiss a woman's hand).

Sense of humor

Romanian humor is earthy and sometimes absurdist or black. Word play and misunderstandings are also universally popular. As an example, this joke is one of many which address hardships during the Communist era: What is colder in a Romanian winter than cold water? Hot water.

Russia

National character

Because religion was suppressed under the Communists, 50 percent of the population consider themselves non-religious, although today many different religions are allowed free expression, including Russian Orthodoxy, Islam, and Judaism. Russians have been accustomed to being closed and collectivistic, dictated by absolute rule. Now they are learning to be more outward looking, individualistic, and objective, although under Vladimir Putin there has been increasing centralization of power and a return to some of the old Communist ways. Free speech, gender equality, and the transition to a free-market economy are substantial issues that will take many years to resolve.

A brief history

A Scandinavian tribe called the Varangians crossed the Baltic Sea and landed in Eastern Europe in the ninth century A.D., where they established a unified, dynastic state in the region that was to become Russia. The Mongols (Tartars) extorted large tax payments out of the region from the thirteenth century onwards, until Peter the Great refused to pay up in 1480 and threw off the Tartar yoke. He was seen by the people as the "gatherer of the Russian lands." Russia became a unified state under the rule of his notorious grandson, Ivan the Terrible. Thirty years after his death, the Romanov dynasty began its 300-year rule of Russia; this ended with the Bolshevik Revolution in 1917, and the creation of the Soviet Union.

The early years after the revolution saw a partial return to a market economy under Lenin, which allowed the country to rebuild its infrastructure. When Lenin died in 1924, however, Stalin took control, collectivization began, and thirty years of brutal repression followed. After World War II, despite an enormous loss of life, Russia emerged as one of the two world powers, along with the United States, and Stalin remained in power until 1953. After his death, political repression relaxed a little but the country stagnated until the 1970s. In March of 1985 Mikhail Gorbachev became general secretary and introduced policies of glasnost (openness) and perestroika (restructuring). In 1991 hard-line apparatchiks who wanted the Soviet motherland to remain intact led an unsuccessful coup against him, and their failure marked the beginning of the end of Communism in Russia, cumulating in the eventual break up of the Soviet Union on December 25, 1991. Today Russia is known as the Russian Federation, and is a multiparty federal republic.

Speaking

Russian is the official language. About one in

five Russians can speak English well enough to hold a conversation.

Russians are traditionally very wary of strangers, with good reason—a habit from the old Communist era that has been hard to break (especially since current president Vladimir Putin appears to be headed in an anti-democratic direction). They are learning to be open, but allow plenty of time for relationships and mutual trust to develop gradually. Despite their initial reserve, Russians are very hospitable and generous.

Safe topics of conversation are sports (especially winter sports), literature, the arts, and weather, which are neutral topics in most cultures. Avoid talking about religion, politics, history, and the relative poverty of Russia compared to the West.

Don't lose your temper: patience is a virtue that Russians hold in spades. Speak in a soft voice; speaking or laughing loudly in public is considered rude.

The OK sign and gestures involving shaking the fist are considered vulgar. However, the thumbs-up gesture indicating approval is acceptable.

Body language

The most common greeting is a firm hand-shake—men and women should take off their right glove to make skin-on-skin contact, no matter how cold it is—with good eye contact. Shaking hands or kissing across the threshold in a doorway is considered very bad luck (in Russian folklore, the doorway was consid-ered the place of the house spirit). Other-wise physical contact between strangers is limited, although hugs, backslaps, and kisses on the cheeks are very common among close friends.

Smiling is not used as a social lubricant since it is considered to be forced—a "smile on duty"—and therefore insincere. Smiling is generally reserved for when something amusing happens. Also, smiling is considered inappropriate when someone is doing some-thing serious, such as work or study. Russian parents tell their children, "Don't smile, be serious at school, and when grown-ups are talking to you!"

Don't point with your finger; use your whole hand. It is unlucky to whistle indoors (in Rus-sian folklore it is believed to bring poverty). If you were to whistle your approval after a play in the theater, Russians would think you were expressing disapproval (their equivalent of booing).

It is traditional to always propose a toast when drinking, and it is impolite to decline an offer of vodka in certain circumstances (such as a funeral banquet). When getting a refill, your glass should stay on the table.

Before leaving on a long journey, all the assembled company will sit in reflective thought for a minute or two before leav-ing the house. Farewells are invested with greater significance here than in the West, and the pause for thought is a manifestation of this.

Sense of humor

Jokes are welcome at any stage in a relation-ship, and help to break the ice. Anecdotes are very popular, especially those that poke fun at politicians and other public figures.

Brezhnev gives his radio address to the Rus-sian people: "Comrades! I have some good news and some bad news. The bad news is that during the next seven years we will eat nothing but garbage. The good news is that there will be plenty for everyone."

Saudi Arabia

National character

Daily life in Saudi Arabia is governed by Islam and the Koran, and visitors to the country should be aware that they are bound by the same Shariah laws as everyone else. Identity and pride comes from one's family and lineage, and the honor of the extended family, as well as from absolute obedience to Islamic principles. Men and women are viewed as very different in terms of their degree of intellect and emotion, and Saudi women continued to face severe discrimination in all aspects of their lives, including the family, education, employment, and the justice system. Foreign women should wear clothes that cover their collarbones and knees and are not figure-hugging. Alcohol, pork, and pornography are strictly forbidden, and crime is almost non-existent due to severe punishments such as amputations for theft and public beheadings for capital offenses. Respect and friendship are held in high esteem, and Saudi hospitality and friendliness are legendary.

A brief history

The Arabian Peninsula has been inhabited for thousands of years, but the country of Saudi Arabia was founded in 1932 when Abdul Aziz Bin Abdul Rahman Al-Saud unified its various nomadic tribes and became its first king. The discovery of oil at Dhahran in 1938 and the revenue it generated allowed King Ibn Saud to begin a massive modernization program, which marked the beginning of this country's special relationship with the United States. Saudi Arabia supported the Allies during World War II (there was a U.S. air base at Dhahran), and gave Egypt financial aid during the Suez crisis in 1956. It was a founding member of the Organization of the Petroleum Exporting Countries (OPEC) in 1960, which controls oil availability and prices. The First Gulf War in 1991 was a big blow to Saudi Arabia, which allowed the stationing of thousands of foreign troops on its soil. After the September 11, 2001, terrorist attacks, the country was shocked to discover that most of the terrorists were Saudi nationals. Today Saudi Arabia remains one of the most wealthy and important oil-producing countries in the world. It is an Islamic monarchy, with the king as both head of state and the head of government and an appointed Council of Ministers advises him (the majority of government officials are members of the King's family).

Speaking

The official language is Arabic, and English is the most popular second language.

In common with many Arab countries, Saudi Arabia is a high-context culture, which means that communication relies on the subtleties of body language, facial cues, subtext, and other forms of nonverbal communication. You should focus on what is not said as much as what is said. Even silence sends an important message.

Starting with the most senior person, greet everyone in the room with a handshake and say "Assalaam Alaikum" (May peace be upon you), to which the response is "Waalaikum As-salaam" (And peace also upon you).

Embracing is common between close friends of the same sex, and women also greet each other with a handshake or a hug. Men should only greet or touch women if they are blood relatives.

Before getting down to business, greetings are followed by prolonged small talk, and inquiries about health and family; this builds trust and is an important part of Arab interaction and it should not be skipped or rushed. If you join a group which is already talking, your host will explain the subject and invite your opinion. Don't change the subject of the conversation unless you are invited to. Express your views plainly and honestly. As long as you argue your case eloquently, your contribution will be appreciated—as intelligent debate is encouraged—so long as it remains polite and respectful.

Don't bring up the subject of a man's wife or female members of his family, even to politely inquire about their health. It is illegal to criticize Islam or the Saudi royal family, or to publicly practice any other religion except Islam (wearing symbols of other religions, such as a crucifix, is forbidden).

Body language
Eat, drink, pass food, and gesture with the right hand only. The left hand is reserved for unclean purposes such as visiting the bathroom. This is because Arabs believe that using toilet paper or wetted toilet paper to wipe is not hygienic enough, so they use their left hand (without paper) while pouring water onto their backside from a receptacle held in the right hand.

Personal space is small. Saudis of the same gender stand close, and there may be more physical contact than you are used to—but don't back away; they will think you are being

reserved (or unfriendly) and will quickly close the gap. Maintain good eye contact.

Saudi friends or family members of the same sex often walk hand-in-hand. If a Saudi of the same sex as you takes your hand it is a sign of friendship.

Don't point with an index finger: use an open hand instead. Don't use the thumbs-up gesture (it is obscene), the OK sign (it means the "evil eye"), or show the soles of your feet (they are dirty, so should be kept out of sight).

Never walk in front of a Muslim who is praying; it is considered a huge insult because it blocks the path between him and Mecca.

Sense of humor
Saudis do not talk about sex and it isn't the subject of jokes. Never make jokes about Islam: in 1993 eighteen-year-old Hadi Al-Mutaif made a joke about Muhammad and has been in prison ever since (he was initially sentenced to death). Do not use sarcasm or critical humor unless you know someone very well and are sure that they won't take offense. The safest policy is to make self-effacing jokes that are clean and uncontroversial.

Singapore

National character

Singapore's population of nearly four million is comprised of 75 percent Chinese, 14 percent Malays, and nearly eight percent Indians. Singapore prides itself on tolerance and integration of its various cultures. Its people are very hard working and meritocratic, and self-restraint is highly prized. Self-esteem is related to wealth, education, and seniority. Society is still quite male-oriented, but gender equality is slowly improving. Punctuality is important.

A brief history

In 1819 this "island at the end of a peninsula," as Singapore was named by a Chinese account in the third century A.D., was annexed by the British, who established a trading post there under the control of Sir Stamford Raffles. It soon became a lucrative asset, and in 1824 a treaty ceded the island completely to the British. It became the center of government for the Straits Settlements, comprised of Malacca, Penang, and Singapore, under the control first of British India, then the Colonial Office in London.

After the opening of the Suez Canal in 1869, Singapore experienced unprecedented prosperity. It became an important crossroads between Europe and East Asia, as well as the main export center in the world for rubber. Singapore fell under Japanese occupation during World War II, and after liberation became part of the British Commonwealth. Self-government was granted in 1959 and the People's Action Party (PAP) took the majority of seats in the Legislative Assembly, which it has kept ever since. In 1963 Singapore joined the Malaysian Federation (which comprised Malaya, Singapore, Sarawak, and North Borneo), but withdrew two years later. It initially struggled to survive as an independent nation, but capitalism was given free rein and a massive industrialization program brought further prosperity. Its disparate population of immigrants was successfully educated and homogenized. It also built up a modern defense force with compulsory national service. It is a parliamentary democracy, although it has been ruled by one party since independence.

Speaking

Singapore has four official languages: Malay, Tamil, Chinese, and English.

Singaporeans are very diplomatic and are reluctant to say "No." Instead, they will often say something like "Perhaps," or "I'll consider it." Saving face is very important in Singapore, so people are ever trying to avoid situations of potential embarrassment.

The best way to get to know someone is to show great interest in their family and children, although not the female members.

Adopt a moderate tone of voice; speaking too loudly is considered rude.

Body language
Greet with a light handshake lasting several seconds. Eye contact is less pronounced than in the West, and prolonged eye contact is seen as confrontational. The traditional Malay greeting between members of the same sex involves touching the hand lightly and then bringing it back to touch the heart. The traditional Indian greeting is a namaste: bow slightly at the waist while holding your palms together below your chin.

Don't touch someone during conversation unless you know them and their preferences very well. Many Singaporean Malays are Muslim, so they avoid all physical contact between the sexes. A Muslim man must ritually cleanse himself before prayer if he has touched a woman. Public affection among same-sex adult friends and relations is commonplace. Many Singaporean Indians are Hindu and also avoid touching between the sexes.

Public displays of affection between members of the opposite sex are inappropriate, even between husband and wife.

Among Muslims and Hindus, the left hand is reserved for unclean uses, such as going to the bathroom. Eat, pass objects, and only touch other people with your right hand.

Do not show the soles of your feet or allow them to touch someone else. Never touch someone's head, not even to pat a child. Avoid standing with your hands on your hips as this is an aggressive gesture.

Sense of humor
Humor is appropriate in most situations and during a first meeting, but put-downs, irony, and sarcasm should be avoided, as well as jokes that criticize the government. Jokes about technology are popular, for example: After digging to a depth of 100 meters, Russian scientists discovered traces of copper wiring dating back 1,000 years, and concluded that their ancestors had a telephone network one thousand years ago.

The following week American scientists discovered traces of 2,000-year-old optical fibers at a depth of 200 meters and concluded that their ancestors already had advanced high-tech digital telephone a millennium earlier than the Russians.

One week later, this report appeared in the Singapore press: "After digging as deep as 500 meters, Singapore scientists have found absolutely nothing. They have concluded that 5,000 years ago, their ancestors were already using mobile phones."

South Africa

National character

South Africa is a culturally diverse country known as the "rainbow nation," full of driven and ambitious people who value individual achievement and appreciate the concept of rags-to-riches.

Of the forty-seven million South Africans, about thirty-seven million are black (divided into four major ethnic groups: Nguni, Sotho, Shangaan-Tsonga, and Venda), five million white, four million colored (the term "colored" in South Africa refers to a heterogeneous group of people who possess some degree of sub-Saharan ancestry, but not enough to be considered Black under South African law), and one million Indian and Asian. While the ruling African National Congress enjoys 70 percent of the national vote, a substantial number of black rural inhabitants still lead largely impoverished lives. The white minority lifestyle and culture is akin to that of Great Britain, although it is considerably more male-dominated. South Africans are generally gregarious and welcoming and the culture is quite laid-back.

A brief history

Humans have inhabited South Africa for 100,000 years. The oldest surviving groups are the San (the Bushmen) and the Khoi-khoi (the Hottentots).

Europeans first arrived in South Africa with Portuguese explorer Bartholomew Dias in the late fifteenth century. The Dutch East India Company established the first European settlement in 1652. Some of these farmers went deeper within the country to become the Boers. After the Napoleonic Wars, Great Britain took control of the Dutch colony in 1795.

In the late nineteenth century the discovery of gold and diamonds sent a huge influx of miners into the Boers' territory, and the British annexation of the Transvaal precipitated the Boer War in 1899. After the Union of South Africa in 1910 the Boers used their political power to oppress the black population, leading to the racial segregation of blacks and whites, known as apartheid.

The African National Congress (ANC) fought against apartheid for decades, and after it was outlawed in 1960 it resorted to violent struggle, while the international community imposed economic sanctions. Finally apartheid was dismantled during the 1990s, and ANC president Nelson Mandela was freed after spending twenty-seven years imprisoned on Robben Island. In 1994 he became the first President of South Africa to be elected in fully-representative democratic elections.

Speaking

English is the most widely spoken European language, followed by Afrikaans, derived from Dutch, which is the mother tongue of 60 percent of the white population and is also spoken by many blacks. There are nine Bantu languages with official status spoken, and many urban blacks speak several indigenous languages. "Hello" is "Sawubona" in Ndebele, Swazi, and Zulu; "Molo" in Xhosa; "Lumela" in Basotho; "Dumela" in Sepedi and Tswana; "Ndaa" (said by a man) and "Aah" (said by a woman) in Venda; and "Minjhani" (when greeting adults) or "Kunjhani" (when greeting your peer group or below your age) in Tsonga.

Maintain a quiet voice in conversation. Raising your voice is considered rude and challenging. Don't yell across the street to attract someone's attention and do not interrupt a South African while they are speaking.

You will often hear the expressions "now-now" and "just now." The former means "immediately" and the latter means at some point later today.

When asking directions, if someone tells you

to "turn left at the robot" they are referring to traffic lights.

The Afrikaans word "Ja," is used as a contraction of "Yes." "How's it?" is a common greeting between English speakers.

Body language

Greeting styles differ between ethnic groups, but when dealing with foreigners, most South Africans shake hands while maintaining eye contact (in black culture it is a sign of respect not to look you in the eye). Some women will not shake hands, but merely nod their head. A kiss on the cheek is used between close friends.

The "African handshake" involves slipping a free hand around the other person's thumb, and is used between blacks and whites and between blacks, but not between whites. If someone supports their arm while shaking hands, or approaches you with their hands together, palms facing out and slightly curled, they are showing respect and deference.

Although the country has a relaxed and informal atmosphere, the culture can include a refined formality. For example, men stand up when women or a senior man enter the room. Men generally will allow women to go first into a room and open the door for them,

although in black culture the opposite is true, as the men go first in case of danger.

Do not show the soles of your feet, or move anything with your feet. The foot is considered unclean. Remove your shoes when entering someone's house, but when sitting keep your feet flat on the floor. Receive gifts with the right hand.

Sense of humor

The white South Africans tend to adopt the British sense of irony, and the blacks align themselves with black American humor culture. South African jokes make use of a named Afrikaans stereotype of stupidity: van der Merwe. For example: Van der Merwe was watching a rugby test against the British Lions at Loftus Versfeld stadium in Pretoria. There was only one empty seat—next to Van der Merwe. "Whose seat is that?" asked his neighbor. "It's for my wife," replies Van der Merwe. "Where is she?" "She died." "So why didn't you give the ticket to one of your friends?" "They've all gone to the funeral."

Spain

National character

Spaniards are tolerant, easy going, and friendly. Independent, proud, and national-istic, Spaniards are fiercely egalitarian: everyone is created equal and is unique, and the humble poor boy who makes good and turns himself into a success is a defining national myth. Individual independence is important, but the family is very important. Relation-ships and the enjoyment of life come before everything else.

Although Spain does not have an official religion, all but 5 percent of the country is Catholic, and religion is deeply embedded in the national psyche. There is also a great respect for authority.

Spaniards have entrenched opinions, and although they are open to new ideas, they take a good deal of persuasion to change their atti-tudes, and are very sensitive to criticism. They can be quite emotional and subjective in their reasoning, so when speaking try to appeal to these qualities, rather then logic. Consider-ations such as promptness are a low priority, and it is not unusual for a Spaniard to be half an hour late to an appointment, and social events rarely start on time. Spanish bureau-

cracy is second to none, and is often exasperatingly drawn out. The Spanish are famous for their concept of mañana, which means "tomorrow," since life in Spain is unhurried.

A brief history

The first settlers in Spain were Iberians, Celts and Basques, followed by conquering the Romans, Moors, and Visigoths. Spain didn't become united as a country until the fifteenth century, when it embarked on the creation of a colonial empire. It became a major worldwide force during the next two centuries, and then gradually lost its empire, until just a few African colonies remained.

The Spanish Civil War of 1936 to 1939 resulted in the deaths of 350,000 people and led to the dictatorship of General Francisco Franco, who ruled until he died in 1975. In 1969 he declared Prince Juan Carlos the future king, who took power after Franco's death. He suppressed a military coup and the first free elections in forty years took place in 1977 and have continued ever since. Spain joined NATO in 1982 and the EU in 1986.

Spain has a considerable artistic and architectural heritage that includes El Greco, Diego Velasquez, Francisco Goya, Pablo Picasso, Joan Miró and Salvador Dalí; and from Roman ruins to the Modernist creations of Antoni Gaudi.

Speaking

The official language is Spanish (or Castilian), but there are several regional languages including Basque, Galician, and Catalan.

Spaniards like to give friendly advice to each other, and even to strangers, so don't be offended is someone appears to be pushing their nose into your business.

Conversation is often very loud and animated with much hand gesturing.

Pay attention to distinct characteristics of Castilian, Galician, Basque, Catalan, Asturian, and Andalusian cultures.

Body language
Spanish body language is among the most explicit of all countries. Expect larger-than-life facial expressions and much hand and arm gesturing. In fact, observing two Spaniards conversing some distance away, you would be forgiven for thinking that they were having an argument.

Eye contact is strong and prolonged. While people don't actually stare at each other, sometimes it's a close call.

Although initial introductions are quite formal, Spanish men who know each other are very tactile with each other, and will often greet and say goodbye with a back slap or a bear hug (abrazo). Women also lightly embrace and kiss the air while touching cheeks.

Personal space is very small so don't back away if a Spaniard stands too close to you or pats your arm or shoulder.

To beckon someone, turn your palm to the floor and wiggle your fingers or even your whole hand.

Spaniards snap their hand downwards for emphasis.

Avoid using the OK sign which is considered rude.

It is rude to yawn or stretch in public.

A Spaniard will judge you more on your body language and congeniality than on what you say, or your perceived status.

Sense of humor
In social situations, the focus of humor is more about sharing a brash and sometimes often low-brow or politically incorrect joke where everyone laughs at the punch line. Spaniards tend to avoid engaging in witty asides or put-downs which would be considered snooty, rude, and sarcastic (although making fun of the French and Germans is ever popular). Don't take yourself too seriously. The Spanish sense of humor is direct and open; think more about belly laughs than making wry observations.

Sweden

National character

Swedes value quality over quantity; there is a high level of consensus and social responsibility. Sweden has one of the best social security systems in the world (and high taxes to pay for it). They are quietly nationalistic and fiercely egalitarian, and dislike those who try to pull rank or show off their wealth. Swedes are informal and welcoming of strangers. They are objective and analytical thinkers who are open to new influences and are very tolerant of alternative viewpoints. Quality of life and the environment are top priorities. Punctuality is very important. Swedes work hard, but the balance between family and work are central (they make it work, rather than just paying lip-service to it). Gender discrimination is among the lowest in Europe as well. The men have a quiet masculinity (the polar opposite of machismo), and both parents really do share the responsibilities of childcare.

A brief history

All Scandinavians trace their ancestry back to the Vikings, who conducted raids on northern Europe from the eighth to eleventh centuries. Originally Denmark was the dominant power in the region. In 1389 the Union of Kalmar united Sweden with Denmark and Norway under the rule of Queen Margaret I of Denmark, but Sweden left the union in 1448. It was conquered briefly by Denmark in 1520, but Sweden regained its independence three years later under Swedish hero Gustav Vasa, who broke with the Roman Catholic Church and established the Protestant Reformation.

Sweden became a great power in the seventeenth century, winning wars against Denmark-Norway, Russia, and Poland, and acquiring important territories in Denmark and Norway. However, Swedish power declined after Peter the Great of Russia defeated the Swedes at the battle of Poltava in 1709. A century later Sweden lost Finland to Russia, but Norway was given to Sweden in 1814 by the Congress of Vienna. Norway broke away from Sweden in 1905. Sweden was neutral in both World Wars and joined the European Union in 1995. Today it is a parliamentary state under a constitutional monarchy, with a king as chief of state and a prime minister as head of the government.

Speaking

It is illegal to discipline children physically, so Swedish parents are very skilled at connecting with their children using verbal reasoning and understanding, and they manage to stay admirably calm at the same time. Losing your temper, especially with your children, is considered very distasteful. Swedes dislike confrontation of any sort, and will avoid it wherever possible.

Keep your voice at a moderate level and avoid loud or rowdy behavior.

Body language

Greet men and women with short, firm hand-shakes on arrival and departure. Always maintain good eye contact. Close friends may hug and kiss. Younger people tend not to shake hands, but may cheek-kiss (not two men).

Swedes consider outward displays of emotion (especially anger) to be unacceptable.

They pride themselves on maintaining their composure in the most trying of circumstances.

Gestures are minimal and Swedes are not tactile. Try to communicate verbally rather than relying heavily on facial and hand gestures. Also, do not touch, backslap, or use any other "buddy" gestures unless you know someone very well.

Sense of humor

Swedes have a very dry sense of humor and often tell jokes with a straight face, and there are few topics that are off limits. Humor is a distraction in the business setting, and is usually considered inappropriate. Here is a popular Swedish joke about Norway, which plays on the idea that Norwegians look down on Swedes: "What does Norway have that Sweden doesn't? Good neighbors."

Switzerland

National character

The Swiss enjoy the highest standard of living on the planet through their pragmatism, hard work, and consensus-building. The culture is very conservative, and people are very reluctant to improvise or change things or beliefs that have appeared to serve them well.

Swiss people appreciate cleanliness, orderliness, planning, hard work, and their material rewards. Great respect is shown to superiors and the elderly. They are very law abiding and value directness and honesty. There is considerable pressure to conform, and punctuality is important—trains and buses run on time, and so do the people. It is not unusual for someone to call if they are going to be five minutes late.

Everyone is expected to be a "giver" who contributes to society rather than expect help from others—the "takers"—so social security is very basic. The Swiss are proud of their neutrality and promotion of worldwide peace. They are also very concerned about the environment, and are second only to Germany in their environmental restrictions.

A brief history

Switzerland has been inhabited for thousands of years. When it was colonized by the Romans it was known as Helvetia. The origins of the Swiss Confederation date back to 1291 when the cantons of Uri, Schwyz, and Unterwalden united against the Habsburgs. Since 1848, the Swiss Confederation has been a federal state of twenty-eight relatively autonomous cantons.

Switzerland's borders were fixed by the Congress of Vienna in 1815 when its neutrality was established, and in 1848 a federal constitution was drawn up. It remained neutral during the two World Wars, but there was a lot Swiss compliance with Nazi Germany, and much Jewish money remained frozen in Swiss bank accounts until recently, when the Swiss were reluctantly obliged to refund large sums of money to descendants.

Speaking

Switzerland has three official languages: French (in the southwest), Italian (about 10 percent of the population, concentrated in the Ticino region in the south), and German (spoken throughout the country). There is also a fourth protected language called Romansch, spoken by about 1 percent of the population.

The Swiss can seem quite formal and reserved at first (especially the German speakers), but will relax with better acquaintance. They are good listeners, and rarely interrupt each other. They are direct communicators who prefer to say what they mean rather than being polite for the sake of it. For example, saying "We must do this again sometime" will be taken very literally as a genuine invitation for another meeting. They take a long time to form personal relationships, but they are honest, responsible, and loyal companions. Over-familiarity too early in a relationship is considered superficial and is viewed with distrust.

Privacy is important, so avoid asking about occupation, age, politics, marital status, income, etc. Religion is also a private matter that is rarely discussed in public. Good topics of conversation are sports, travel, cuisine, and aspects of Switzerland that have impressed you.

Body language
The handshake is the standard greeting throughout Switzerland. French Swiss or Italian Swiss people may kiss and hug.

You will be judged on your appearance and your body language, so dress well and be well groomed or you won't be taken seriously.

Keep your hands out of your pockets, espe-cially when talking. Also, do not stretch or slouch in public.

Do not sit with one ankle resting on the other knee.

Sense of humor
The Swiss enjoy an understated repartee that requires a sharp and intelligent wit which elicits smiles rather than loud belly laughs. Avoid critical banter as it is likely to be taken literally and cause offense. There's little room for humor in business, which is serious and efficient; making jokes in a business environ-ment is viewed as childish and disruptive. An example of Swiss humor: "In Heaven the cooks are French, the lovers are Italian, the mechanics are German, the police are British, and the whole place is run by the Swiss. In Hell the cooks are British, the lovers are Swiss, the mechanics are French, the police are German, and the whole place is run by the Italians."

Taiwan

National character

Taiwan is a modern country and one of the wealthiest in East Asia. Ninety percent of its inhabitants are Buddhist, Confucian, or Taoist.

To say its people are hard working is an understatement: work is their purpose in life, since the accumulation of wealth is the single most important aspiration. Loyalty, obedience to the family, and business organization are paramount. Maintaining face, not causing

anyone else to lose face, and avoiding bringing dishonor to the family are also important. Society is male-dominated, and punctuality is highly regarded, as are modesty, sincerity, and honesty.

A brief history

The original inhabitants of Taiwan were Austronesian, and migration into the country from China began in the sixth century. The Dutch colonized Taiwan during the seventeenth century; Spanish traders briefly settled in the north, but were driven out by the Dutch. In 1662 Ming loyalists escaped the Manchu invasion which established the Qing (Ch'ing) dynasty, by fleeing to Taiwan and taking control there. In 1895 Taiwan fell under Japanese control after the First Sino-Japanese War, but it was returned to China after World War II. The Kuomintang or Chinese Nationalist Party (KMT) rule of Taiwan was repressive and corrupt, so violence broke out on February 28, 1947, between the Taiwanese and their mainlander rulers. The Nationalists cracked down hard on the island, killing more than 30,000 Taiwanese and imprisoning many more. This incident has left deep scars in the relationship between Taiwan and mainland China. When the Communist Party of China (CPC) led by Mao Tse-tung finally defeated the KMT in 1949, about two million KMT refugees fled to Taiwan, and set up Nationalist rule there. Resentment and controversy still surround the issue of Taiwan becoming a separate independent state. In 2000, the Democratic Progressive Party (DPP) candidate Chen Shui-bian was elected president of Taiwan, becoming the first non-KMT member to rule Taiwan since 1945. Today the country's official name is Republic of China, and it is often referred to as Nationalist China.

Speaking

The official language is Mandarin Chinese, and Taiwanese and Hakka dialects are also spoken.

Trust in relationships is built up slowly, so don't switch to a first name basis until invited.

Compliments will be deflected with a modest comment such as "It was nothing," rather than the more direct "Thank you" common in Western cultures. Likewise, when you are thanking someone, don't make too big a deal of it, as you will cause embarrassment. However genuine compliments are always appreciated, although you should not admire other people's possessions or they may feel obliged to give them to you.

In the West the conversation at mealtimes can flow around a wide range of topics from sport to politics. In Taiwan it is focused almost entirely on the food, with frequent compliments to the host, and frequent toasting, which the host initiates with the words "Gan bei" or "Dry the glass," after which everyone drains their drinks.

The Taiwanese are very diplomatic and are reluctant to say "No." Instead, they will most likely say something like "Perhaps," or "I'll consider it." Saving face is very important in

Taiwan, so people are ever looking to avoid situations of potential embarrassment.

Expect to be asked lots of personal questions such as how much you earn or how much you paid for something. This is perfectly acceptable in Taiwan. Avoid discussing Taiwan's political relationship with mainland China. If someone offers you a gift, it is customary to refuse the offer three times before finally accepting it (the Western equivalent of "You really shouldn't have!").

Body language

The traditional Taiwanese greeting is a bow or nod of the head. Greeting someone is taken seriously, and may be with a straight face, without a smile. Keep eye contact brief. If you shake hands, the grip is much lighter than in the West. Using a firm handshake is likely to be seen as pushy and aggressive.

Keep your hand gestures to a minimum, as Taiwanese people find them distracting and annoying.

Always allow older people to pass through a doorway before you, even if they refuse; generally defer to seniority. Old people also appreciate a comment on their good health.

Sense of humor

Taiwanese humor is quite juvenile, scatological, often absurdist, and frequently aimed at foreigners (white, black, or Asian, but not Chinese: In 2006 enraged Chinese mainlanders demanded a public apology from a Taiwanese model, Jessey Meng, after she poked fun at their public toilets on a Taiwan chat-show. She observed "Many mainland toilets don't have doors and even when they do, most people don't even shut the door!" and she went on to describe seeing "hundreds of pale bottoms all lined up in a row").

Thailand

National character

Ninety-five percent of the inhabitants are Theravada Buddhists, which focuses upon spiritual liberation of the individual; most of the remainder is Muslim. Their religion provides a liberating rather than restrictive framework in which each individual is encouraged to find their own path and take responsibility for their own thoughts and actions. This makes Thais very open to the feelings of others. At the same time they are mindful of the role that luck and fate play in daily life, so they can accommodate uncertainty easily. Society is very hierarchical, and everyone is expected to fulfill their roles within it with the minimum of upheaval. Patience, tolerance, and self-reliance are important. People are motivated by the activity of karma, rather than money and personal achievement.

A brief history

Originally called Siam, the country has been inhabited for more than 4,000 years. Theravada Buddhism entered the region around the third century A.D. Thriving agricultural communities developed into a loose collection

131

of city states during the Dvaravati period, lasting until the eleventh century when the Kymers invaded. During the thirteenth century, the first true Thai kingdom developed, which at its height stretched from Nakhon Si Thammarat to Vientiane in Laos. This kingdom spread eastward during the next two centuries. The Chakri dynasty began in 1782 with King Rama I, who created the present-day capital at Bangkok. This dynasty lasted until a bloodless coup in 1932 replaced the absolute monarch with a system of constitutional monarchy. Coup leader Phibul Songkhram ruled until the end of World War II, during which Thailand was occupied by the Japanese. The name was changed from Siam to Thailand in 1939. The name "Thailand" means "free land," and it is the only country in Southeast Asia never to have been a European colony. Since 1939 Thailand has had seventeen constitutions and eighteen military coups; the last one in February 1991 toppled the civilian Prime Minister Chatichai Choonhavan as head of the government. The current monarch, King Rama IX (who has maintained his position as head of state, while the many coups replaced the head of the government) is the longest reigning monarch in the world and commands great respect in Thailand as well as abroad.

Speaking

The official language is Thai, which is related to Chinese. Other spoken languages include Chinese, Lao, and Malay.

For "Hello" men say "Sawatdee krup" and women say "Sawatdee kaa."

Speak with a calm voice at all times; if you raise your voice or express anger, you will lose respect and cause embarrassment. Always keep your cool, be polite and respectful, and be ready to apologize if you sense that you have caused offense or committed a breach of etiquette, however minor.

Thais are masters of inferring context, and often what is not said is more important than what is said. Be sensitive to the subtleties of nonverbal communication. For example, a Thai nod means "I respect your authority, I respect you." It does not mean yes.

There is no independent word for "No" in Thai, only "Not-yes" (mai chai).

It is illegal to criticize any member of the royal family, even as a joke, and you should show respect towards anything that bears their face, such as stamps and currency. It is also an offense to insult any religion, including Buddhism.

Body language

The standard greeting is a wai: the palms are pressed together as if in prayer with arms and elbows held close to the body, accompanied by a bow of the head that meets your fingers. The height of the hands during the bow depends on the status of the other person. When performing a wai to an equal, the hands should be at chest level; to monks and elders the hands are at nose- or forehead-level. Buddha is waied with hands above the head. Do not wai children or service staff, just nod slightly. The wai is also used for saying goodbye.

Don't touch a monk; when introduced to one, make a verbal greeting without shaking hands.

All images of the Buddha are considered sacred, so you must act appropriately towards them: do not touch, point your feet toward, turn your back on, stand higher than, or pose for photographs in front of a Buddha. When walking away from a Buddha, take two or three steps back while still facing it, then after bowing lightly you may turn around.

Never touch anyone on the head, even a child, and apologize immediately if you do.

Any public displays of affection greater than holding hands are inappropriate.

Do not point your foot at anyone, or cross your legs in front of an older person.

Beckon with the outstretched palm down and waggle the fingers towards the body.

Sense of humor

Thailand is known as the "Land of Smiles," so friendliness, humor, and laughter are an integral part of daily life. However, be sensitive to the fact that laughter is also used to cover embarrassment, and it is important to remember that smiles are also used as an apology.

Turkey

National character

Turkey is in a unique position as a bridge between the East and the West. While most of the population is Sunni Muslim, the state is fiercely secular, so women are allowed to take a prominent role in public life and enjoy significantly more gender equality than their Arab neighbors. Individual expression and involvement is more important than subjugation to laws or to Islam. The family and national pride are important social binders, and society is very hierarchical, with elders commanding a lot of respect.

A brief history

The Republic of Turkey was the successor state of the Ottoman Empire, following its dissolution after World War I. Sultan Mehmet VI Vahdettin was replaced by a new Republican assembly on October 29, 1923. Mustafa Kemal (Atatürk) became the country's first president. Turkey joined the League of Nations in July 1932. It signed a peace treaty with Germany and remained neutral during World War II, joined NATO in 1952, and allied itself with the West during the Cold War. During the First Gulf War in 1991, Turkey supported Kuwait instead of its neighbor and important trading partner, Iraq. The country suffered economically as a result. In 2003 Turkey did not take part in the invasion of Iraq. Today it is a multiparty democracy, a secular state with no official religion. It has been trying to become a member of the EEC/EU for forty years, but is currently blocked because of human rights concerns (in particular the EU has called on Turkey to improve its freedom of speech), its refusal to open its ports and airports to traffic from EU member Cyprus, and a feeling among certain EU countries that Turkey just isn't culturally "European" enough.

Speaking

"Merhaba" is "Hello" and "Nasilsiniz" means "How are you?" The usual reply to this is "Elyiyim teshekur ederim" (Fine, thank you).

Greet everyone in the room with a firm handshake with good eye contact, starting with the oldest. With some elders it is customary to greet them by kissing their hand and then touching it to your forehead. Close friends of either sex may use a two-handed handshake with a kiss on each cheek. Men should wait for a woman to extend her hand before shaking it, since strict Muslims avoid physical contact between members of the opposite sex.

A good topic of conversation is to ask someone about their family. Soccer and wrestling are very popular. Avoid discussing ethnic conflicts such as those with the Greeks and Kurds.

Body language

Turks rely on a lot of body language and gestures. Shaking the head means "I don't understand," not "No." Nod to say "Yes"; raise your eyebrows accompanied by a "Tsk" sound, or tilt your head back slightly, to say "No."

Avoid public displays of affection with members of the opposite sex, including hugging, kissing, and holding hands.

Stand up when an elder enters the room.

To attract someone's attention wave up-and-down rather than from side to side.

It is rude to cross your arms when facing someone. Don't show the soles of your feet: keep them flat on the ground when sitting.

Poking the thumb between the index and middle fingers of a clenched fist is obscene.

Sense of humor

Turkish humor can involve double-entendre, but don't make explicit references to sex. Avoid sarcasm or critical humor unless you know someone very well and are sure that they won't take offense, and even then, be tactful.

United Kingdom

National character

Although many people would argue that the British class system is all but gone, the majority of the population still refers to themselves as either working class or middle class. Increasingly status has little to do with wealth or aspirations, but is linked to a person's job. For example, a typical university lecturer would call himself middle class, even though his earnings are considerably less than that of a plumber, who would generally call himself working class. Status is still primarily based on power and wealth, although overt displays of wealth are considered vulgar. Britain prides itself on being a tolerant society, and most citizens (religious groups aside) believe that all forms of individual expression are acceptable so long as they don't disturb or upset others. Although they have an international reputation for being uptight and snobbish, most Brits are informal and fun-loving, with good work ethics and strong family values.

A brief history

Originally occupied by Celts, the island was invaded by the Romans in the first century A.D., who then ruled until the fifth century. After the Romans left, other tribes invaded, including the Angles, Saxons, and Jutes. In 1066 the Normans invaded from France,
beating King Harold at the decisive Battle of Hastings. The Normans turned most of the region into a feudal kingdom. The Magna Carta of 1215 required the king to renounce certain rights and accept that the will of the king could be bound by law. The country has had a monarchy ever since, apart from a brief spell during the middle of the seventeenth century when Oliver Cromwell presided over a republic.

By the nineteenth century Britain was the strongest power in Europe, with a huge worldwide empire. The current monarchy, the House of Windsor, came into being in 1917. Britain's empire diminished during the first half of the twentieth century as it granted independence first to New Zealand, Australia, and Canada, then to India, Egypt, and the African colonies after World War II.

The United Kingdom is a political union made up of four constituent countries: England, Scotland, Wales, and Northern Ireland. The official religion is the Anglican Church, or Church of England.

Speaking

On first meeting shake the person's hand (try to match the pressure of that individual) with good eye contact and say, "How do you do?" or the less formal, "Pleased to meet you." In more casual circumstances, a group wave and

"Hi" are acceptable. Women and friends of the opposite sex may hug and air-kiss above one or more cheeks.

At social events you will be judged on your social confidence and your ability to contribute to the conversation in an intelligent and informed way. Contrary to popular opinion, the British are not obsessed with talking about the weather—they just prefer it to an awkward silence.

Most people are happy to move to first name terms almost immediately, since using titles is considered uncomfortably formal outside of certain business circles. However, asking direct personal questions such as "What do you do?" is considered gauche, since it suggests that you intend to judge the other person by what they do rather than by who they are.

The British do not use much eye contact while speaking, and it is quite common to hold a conversation while the other person stands at right angles to you and stares off into the distance, only occasionally meeting your gaze; this is a sign of British reserve, rather than aloofness or disinterest.

Body language

The British use a range of non-specific hand gestures to punctuate their speech, but tend to find excessive hand gestures rather comic and excessive.

The thumbs-up gesture indicates approval, but you will rarely see it used in well-educated affluent company. The OK gesture is understood, but rarely used.

Sense of humor

British humor is full of intelligent irony, understatement, and—between closer male friends—banter and put-downs. Humor crops up in just about every situation and is often used in business or social events to break the ice or diffuse tension or embarrassment. The best quality of Brits is their ability to laugh at themselves and their history and traditions, and few targets are off limits, least of all the Monarchy. "Sick" jokes such as "Why was Lady Di's death a tragedy? Because the rest of the Royal Family wasn't in the back of the car with her," are commonplace, but should not be brought up in polite circles.

United States Of America

National character

Americans are generally upbeat and positive, and put their faith in life, liberty, and the pursuit of happiness—the three principles on which the country was founded. While the defining national myth teaches that with hard work and persistence anyone can rise from the bottom to become rich and successful, in reality there is an ever widening gap between rich and poor. Many poorly educated citizens and ethnic minorities are stuck in low-paying jobs with little prospect of improvement. However, everyone is equal under the law. The culture is highly individualistic, and success and the accumulation of wealth are championed. As a result the work ethic is very strong and people tend to define others by their jobs. Americans are very welcoming, outgoing, and friendly, although many have limited knowledge and awareness of other cultures outside their own.

A brief history

The original inhabitants of the U.S. were the indigenous people known as Native Americans. In 1565 the first Europeans (the Spanish) arrived and established St. Augustine, Florida. In 1607 English settlers established the colony of Jamestown in Virginia. In 1620, the Mayflower, the famous ship that trans-

ported the Pilgrims from Plymouth, England, arrived at Plymouth Colony, Massachusetts. During the seventeenth and eighteenth centuries, hundreds of thousands of black slaves were imported from Africa to work on cotton and tobacco plantations. In 1776 the United States was formed after it declared and won its independence from Great Britain, with George Washington as the first president. The constitution was drawn up in 1787.

Between 1861 and 1865, a civil war was fought between the United States Federal government (the "Union") and eleven Southern slave states that declared their secession to form the Confederate States of America. The Confederacy lost, and slavery was abolished.

In 1929 the stock market crash caused the Great Depression, which lasted until Franklin D. Roosevelt's New Deal rescued the economy (although some historians would argue that his policy prolonged the Great Depression). The U.S.'s decision to join the war against Hitler in 1941 was a decisive factor in Germany's eventual defeat. In 1945 the U.S. dropped two atomic bombs on the Japanese cities of Hiroshima and Nagasaki, which hastened the end of the war.

During the 1960s and 1970s, 60,000 U.S. soldiers were killed in the disastrous Vietnam War. On September 11, 2001, 3,000 people were killed when four commercial passenger jets were hijacked by Islamic terrorists. Two

141

of them crashed into the twin towers of the World Trade Center in New York City; one into the Pentagon in Arlington County, Virginia; and the other was brought down near the town of Shanksville in rural Somerset County, Pennsylvania, after the passengers attempted to regained control. Following the attacks President George W. Bush invaded Iraq in 2003, without the approval of the United Nations. This act has further destabilized the Middle East.

Speaking

In business and formal social situations the customary greeting is a very firm handshake with good eye contact. Say "Hello" or "How are you?" and reply with "Hi," or "Fine, thanks." In more informal situations a verbal greeting accompanied by a nod and/or a wave is sufficient.

It is customary to accept compliments by smiling and saying "Thank you," rather than to deflect it by denying the compliment or being self-effacing, as is common in many Eastern cultures. Often compliments are used to initiate a conversation.

Americans often begin a conversation by asking, "What do you do?" In many ways, people in the U.S. are defined by their answers to this question.

Body language

Americans are tactile, and men will often slap each other on the back as a sign of friendship and approval. Public displays of affection are acceptable in most parts of the country.

The standard body space is about two feet, or an arm's length.

To show approval, use either the thumbs-up sign or the OK sign.

Direct eye contact is important as it shows sincerity and trustworthiness.

Sense of humor

The best of American humor is social commentary that is topical and satirical. America has produced some of the world's most popular TV sitcoms, from The Simpsons to Seinfeld. Jokes range from political and cultural values humor to puns and play on words. While Americans understand the concepts of irony and sarcasm, in practice some will take you literally when you attempt to use them.